Friends
of the Lewes Public Library

This book was purchased with funds
provided by the
Friends of Lewes Public Library

New Critical Essays on
Toni Morrison's
GOD HELP THE CHILD

New Critical Essays on
Toni Morrison's
GOD HELP THE CHILD
Race, Culture, and History

Edited by Alice Knox Eaton,
Maxine Lavon Montgomery, and Shirley A. Stave

Lewes Public Library
111 Adams Ave.
Lewes, DE 19958
302-645-2733

University Press of Mississippi / Jackson

The University Press of Mississippi is the scholarly publishing agency of the Mississippi Institutions of Higher Learning: Alcorn State University, Delta State University, Jackson State University, Mississippi State University, Mississippi University for Women, Mississippi Valley State University, University of Mississippi, and University of Southern Mississippi.

www.upress.state.ms.us

The University Press of Mississippi is a member of the Association of University Presses.

Copyright © 2020 by University Press of Mississippi
All rights reserved
Manufactured in the United States of America

First printing 2020

∞

Library of Congress Cataloging-in-Publication Data

Names: Eaton, Alice Knox, editor. | Montgomery, Maxine Lavon, 1959- editor. | Stave, Shirley A., 1952- editor.
Title: New critical essays on Toni Morrison's God help the child: race, culture, and history / edited by Alice Knox Eaton, Maxine Lavon Montgomery, and Shirley A. Stave.
Description: Jackson: University Press of Mississippi, 2020. | Includes bibliographical references and index.
Identifiers: LCCN 2020006523 (print) | LCCN 2020006524 (ebook) | ISBN 9781496828873 (hardback) | ISBN 9781496828880 (trade paperback) | ISBN 9781496828897 (epub) | ISBN 9781496828903 (epub) | ISBN 9781496828910 (pdf) | ISBN 9781496828927 (pdf)
Subjects: LCSH: Morrison, Toni. God help the child. | American literatureAfrican American authors21st centuryHistory and criticism. | BISAC: LITERARY CRITICISM / American / African American | LCGFT: Essays. | Literary criticism.
Classification: LCC PS3563.O8749 N49 2020 (print) | LCC PS3563.O8749 (ebook) | DDC 813/.54dc23
LC record available at https://lccn.loc.gov/2020006523
LC ebook record available at https://lccn.loc.gov/2020006524

British Library Cataloging-in-Publication Data available

Contents

Acknowledgments vii

Introduction ix

Section 1   Old Scars, New Wounds, and the Search for Wholeness

Skin Deep: Identity and Trauma in *God Help the Child* 5
Shirley A. Stave

The Power of Witnessing: Confronting Trauma
in *God Help the Child* 30
Evelyn Jaffe Schreiber

Childhood Traumas, Journeys, and Healing in Toni Morrison's
God Help the Child 47
Mar Gallego

"Let the True Note Ring Out Loud": A Mindful Reading of
God Help the Child 67
Susana Vega-González

Section 2   Subverting Whiteness: Writing beyond the Racialized Gaze

"What Did I Do to Be So Black and Blue?": Synesthesia in
God Help the Child 89
Anissa Wardi

"You Not the Woman I Want": Toni Morrison's *God Help the Child*
and the Legend of Galatea 106
Maxine Lavon Montgomery

Section 3   Intertextual Interceptions

Return of the Repressed: The Politics of Engraving and Erasure
and the Quest for Selfhood in *God Help the Child* 123
Justine Tally

No System of Justice: At the Margins with Toni Morrison's
Intertextual Characters 140
Alice Knox Eaton

Contributors 159

Index 163

Acknowledgments

This volume grew out of a panel, "Not Post, Not Past: Race and the Construction of Female Subjectivity in *God Help the Child*," which the coeditors presented at the International Society for the Study of Narrative Annual Conference, at the University of Amsterdam in June 2016. Our individual papers dovetailed together in interesting and surprising ways, and inspired us to reach out to other scholars writing about Morrison's newest novel. — **M. M.**

Working with Holly and Maxine, in person and (mostly) via email, has been one of the great pleasures of my scholarly career. I would also like to thank my family, Scott, Liza, and the Lenas, for their devotion and support. My student assistant, Anthony Valentino, did crucial work in compiling the index. — **A. E.**

Collaboration is so important in our discipline, and working with Allie and Maxine has been a rich experience for me. I wish to extend my gratitude to the Northwestern State University Foundation for the privilege of taking part in a research retreat at Cypress Bend. I would also like to thank my dear friend Justine Tally for much meaningful conversation about this novel (over glasses of wine and great food), and also my husband, Richard Pool, for putting up with an often distracted and over-busy wife. — **S. S.**

Introduction

In her eleventh novel, *God Help the Child*, Toni Morrison returns to several of the signature themes explored in her previous work: pernicious beauty standards for women, particularly African American women; mother-child relationships; racism and colorism; and child sexual abuse. *God Help the Child*, published in 2015, is set in the contemporary period, unlike all of her previous novels. The contemporary setting is ultimately incidental to the project of the novel, however; as with Morrison's other work, the story takes on mythic qualities, and the larger-than-life themes lend themselves to allegorical and symbolic readings that resonate in light of both contemporary and historical issues.

Our collection of eight essays by seasoned Morrison scholars as well as new and rising scholars takes on the novel in a nuanced and insightful analysis, interpreting the novel in relation to Morrison's earlier work as well as locating it within ongoing debates in literary and other academic disciplines engaged with African American literature. These essays build on previous work on Morrison's novels and deepen readers' understanding of both her newest novel and her larger literary output.

Recent work on Morrison's novels has informed our approach to *God Help the Child*, in particular Jean Wyatt's *Love and Narrative Form in Morrison's Later Novels* and Lucille P. Fultz's *Toni Morrison: Playing with Difference*. In Wyatt, who has written extensively on Morrison, the author again uses psychoanalysis as the theoretical lens through which to explore how love, which she pointedly distinguishes from desire, functions in the structuring of Morrison's narratives. Wyatt maintains that Morrison requires the reader to participate in the creation of the text through her strategy of suspending revelations necessary for establishing narrative coherence. As such, the narratives reveal how the characters are experiencing *Nachtraglichkeit*, the Freudian term for the delayed action in a person's response to an event, often as a result of trauma. However, in the works that come after *Beloved*, Wyatt argues, love becomes the mechanism by which characters are able to move forward from trauma rather than continuing to relive it. Wyatt also maintains that Morrison's narratives employ a form of call-and-response in their demand for readerly involvement in the construction of the text.

Like Wyatt, Fultz focuses on the narrative strategies that Morrison employs that invite the reader to share in the creation of her texts. Fultz argues that readers must read Morrison's work from two positions simultaneously—focusing on the historical time period in which the novel is set as well as on the time in which the author wrote the work, since the texts will provide commentary on both. Fultz explores how Morrison "plays" with her readers and her texts, moving away from a sociological exploration of racial issues to a more nuanced and sophisticated form of narration.

Section One of this collection, *Old Scars, New Wounds, and the Search for Wholeness*, explores the topic of how a subject overcomes the scarring left by a toxic childhood. Morrison has throughout her oeuvre delved into the link between a dysfunctional childhood and a troubled adulthood. In the most extreme cases, such as that of Pecola Breedlove in *The Bluest Eye* or of Sethe in *Beloved*, madness or infanticide results from childhood trauma. In some cases, as with the Convent women in *Paradise*, healing is achieved. In this volume, Shirley A. Stave, in her essay "Skin Deep: Identity and Trauma in *God Help the Child*," focuses on how the characters of Bride and Booker must renegotiate their understanding of how their inability to sustain a meaningful relationship is driven by incidents they experienced as children. Reading the text through the Lacanian matrix of the imaginary and symbolic orders, the essay explores how the two characters have remained fixed in the imaginary, perceiving only their surfaces as having meaning until incidents in their lives propel them toward growth and maturity. The essay employs Judith Butler's work on sexual identity, applying it to race, specifically through the concept of abjection, as well as Lucille Fultz's work on Morrison's construction of a tension between raced identity and individual subjectivity. In her essay "The Power of Witnessing: Confronting Trauma in *God Help the Child*," Evelyn Jaffe Schreiber builds on her work in her study *Race, Trauma, and Home in the Novels of Toni Morrison*, describing Morrison's novel as a "holding place" for African American trauma, calling on storytelling traditions and the importance of witnessing in the healing process. Employing Dori Laub's work on trauma studies, but reaching out to Lacan, as Stave has done, and Kaja Silverman, Schreiber argues that the wounds that both Bride and Booker carry are born from the violence endured by generations of African Americans and are, in that sense, communal rather than individual. Only by relating their stories to each other, and, in the process, truly learning to listen, can they achieve a sense of their own worth and commit to each other and their yet unborn child as mature adults. Mar Gallego's essay "Childhood Traumas, Journeys, and Healing in Toni Morrison's *God Help the Child*" considers how racism and sexism contribute to childhood trauma. Drawing on both gender theory and intersectional studies, specifically the work of Patricia Hill Collins, the essay argues that Morrison creates a scenario through which Bride and Booker can overcome their disabling pasts to forge male and female identities freed from the stereotypical assumptions that have hobbled them, allowing them to arrive at a place of wholeness. In the final essay in this section, "'Let the True Note Ring Out Loud': A Mindful Reading of *God Help the Child*," Susana Vega-Gonzalez reads the novel as a literary manifestation of mindfulness, employing psychiatry and psychology rather than psychoanalysis as Stave and Schreiber do. Vega-Gonzales argues that the narrative encapsulates the maxims of mindfulness: awareness of the present moment, compassion and kindness, love, gratitude, forgiveness, introspection, self-knowledge, understanding, and acceptance. Given the multiple cases of trauma that abound in the novel, the essay maintains that the mindfulness evident throughout Bride's and Booker's internal journeys allows them to channel the memories that haunt and devastate them into healing and inner peace.

In Section Two, *Subverting Whiteness: Writing beyond the Racialized Gaze*, we explore Morrison's formal experimentation in her last novel. Morrison's narratives are always bold and rely on intertextuality to enrich the readerly experience. Whether she is using the Dick and Jane books familiar to older readers from elementary school as a way to explore race and poverty in *The Bluest Eye*, or adapting her prose to perform as a musical composition in *Jazz*, Morrison pushes herself and her readers to engage with her texts in innovative ways. In "'What Did I Do to Be So Black and Blue?': Synesthesia in *God Help the Child*," Anissa Wardi grounds her work in the philosophy of Suzanne Langer as well as Joddy Murray's work on nondiscursive symbolization. Starting with the concept of color field painting, Wardi examines Morrison's description of emotional pain through her startling use of color, using the metaphor of synesthesia (the neurological condition in which human senses can fuse, so that, for example, one can see sound as color). She maintains that Morrison's interjection of color into the narrative intensifies the reader's understanding of the trauma experienced by the characters. Maxine Lavon Montgomery's essay "'You Not the Woman I Want': Toni Morrison's *God Help the Child* and the Legend of Galatea" rounds out this section in an examination of Morrison's use of classical imagery to upend utopian promises offered by twenty-first-century popular culture. Reading through the lens of postcolonial theory and Derridean deconstruction, the essay argues that the novel responds to Ovid's myth in such a way as to call attention to a "raced, trans-national history" and to give voice to the voiceless female subject of the early story.

The final section of this collection, entitled "Intertextual Interceptions," treats the novel's interplay with earlier Morrison texts. Morrison scholars have explored the author's use of intertextuality—for example, her choosing to heal the rupture that severed Sula from Nel in *Sula* through the love stronger than death that unites Christine and Heed in *Love*, and her decisión to conclude *Beloved* with the image of a naked pregnant young woman wandering off into the woods only to have a naked pregnant young woman appear by the side of the road in *Jazz*. Justine Tally's essay "Return of the Repressed: The Politics of Engraving and Erasure and the Quest for Selfhood in

Introduction

God Help the Child" reads the novel against Morrison's earlier novels *The Bluest Eye* and *Beloved*, along with various other texts from literary and popular culture, in an exploration of what it means to memorialize a significant loss, both personally and as a community. Tally points out how both *The Bluest Eye* and *God Help the Child* treat the problematic obsession with physical beauty, specifically in the constitution of subjectivity. She goes on to explore how memory can function as a mechanism for the loss of self unless the subject can connect with others in an ethics of care. In "No System of Justice: At the Margins with Morrison's Intertextual Characters," Alice Eaton focuses on Morrison's fascination with intertextual characters within her own oeuvre, particularly on characters who seem stuck at the margins both in society and in Morrison's own stylistic universe. She begins by exploring Morrison's treatment of mothers who reject their "ugly" daughters, which happens first in *The Bluest Eye* and again in *God Help the Child*. She continues by analyzing the concept of justice as it is framed by the US legal system and considers how Morrison's fictional universe exists in an interplay with that system, understanding that while justice may not exist, healing remains possible.

God Help the Child has already joined Morrison's other texts on syllabi in colleges and universities around the globe, and we hope these eight essays offer useful critical insights into Morrison's newest novel and its relation to her oeuvre of fiction and nonfiction in its totality.

New Critical Essays on
Toni Morrison's
GOD HELP THE CHILD

Section 1

Old Scars, New Wounds, and The Search for Wholeness

Skin Deep: Identity and Trauma in *God Help the Child*

Shirley A. Stave

Toni Morrison's 2015 novel, *God Help the Child*, raises vexing questions about the construction of identity in the face of childhood trauma inflected through the lens of race. Initially seeming to interrogate the old debate over the social construction of identity vs. essential identity, the novel veers off on a trajectory that plays surface (i.e., skin) off depth (i.e., consciousness). Such an exploration is significant since racism is most obviously predicated upon the color of skin, but permeates the surface to create anxiety about blood, contamination, and impurity. The novel's two main characters, Bride and Booker, both attempt to evade depth, albeit in radically different ways.

Bride, the novel's main character, suffers for the first two decades of her life because of her blue-black skin. Born to very light-skinned parents, with a great-grandmother who abandoned her children to pass as white, Bride herself is "[m]idnight black, Sudanese black" (Morrison 3); at her birth, her mother briefly considers smothering her to death, while her father simply abandons his wife and the infant daughter he is convinced has been fathered by someone else. The issue of the internal color line is one Morrison has explored before,[1] as have other African American novelists. Nella Larson's *Passing*, as its title suggests, treats two women who are capable of passing for white, one who does so on occasion for convenience, the other who has abandoned her family to marry a racist white man who has no clue as to his wife's racial heritage. Zora Neale Hurston's *Their Eyes Were Watching God* features a main character whose light skin and gently waving, silky hair result in another black woman's attempts to encourage her to marry a light-skinned black man rather than to stay with her darker-skinned lover Tea Cake. Toni Morrison's *Paradise* flips the scenario to show the arrogance of a community of blue-black men who reject and demean lighter-skinned black people. However, in many of her other works, Morrison reveals the privilege granted to those capable of passing the paper bag test—Jadine from *Tar Baby* immediately comes to mind—as well as the scorn heaped upon those who are darker, such as Pecola in *The Bluest Eye*. The community of Ruby in *Paradise* notwithstanding, light skin privilege has existed since slavery days, when lighter skin was perceived by slave owners as more European and hence more aesthetically pleasing, the result being that house slaves, whose work load was less onerous and whose lives were less brutal, tended to have lighter skin. Even today, the internal color line vexes many, and the pressure to marry lighter-skinned partners remains a part of racial consciousness.

Ironically, however, Bride's color is problematic within the context of racism, since her body's surface can be read as the vestigial trace of untainted African blood. In her family's dedication to "whitening up," what must remain unacknowledged is the plight of those ancestors who were seen as subhuman because of their color, even as the project of "whitening up" began with the rape of their female progenitors. As Demetrius L. Eudell argues, citing Sylvia Wynter for support, African Americans must come to terms with "the *representation* of those of African hereditary descent, as the ontological lack within the terms [...] of the secularized autopoetic field of meaning of the Judaeo-Christian West" (23, emphasis in original). Hortense Spillers similarly argues that, through the mechanism of slavery, the black woman became "the principal point of passage between the human and the non-human world. Her issue became the focus of a cunning difference—visually, psychologically, ontologically—as the route by which the dominant male decided the distinction between humanity and 'other' [....] In other words, the black person mirrored for the society around her what a human being was *not*" (155, emphasis in original). The horror Bride's mother experiences at her child's color cannot be overstated, since it indicates her confrontation with her repressed knowledge of how her own color marks her as nonhuman in the eyes of some. Sweetness has prided herself on having escaped the onus of virulent racial hatred. Because her grandmother passed for white (abandoning her family in the process), and her own parents gained some privilege through their light color—her mother "wasn't stopped from trying on hats in the department stores or using their ladies' rooms," and her father "could try on shoes in the front part of a shoestore, not in a back room" (4)—Sweetness has claimed a form of "white privilege" not available to darker-skinned African Americans. Bride's color, then, functions as the return of the repressed, the visible marker that demands the acknowledgment of an enslaved past, even as it underscores what Sweetness also would not choose to concede—that her own light skin bespeaks the rape(s) of her foremothers. Similarly, Sweetness's husband abandons his family because he believes Bride's color indicates sexual license on the part of his wife; paradoxically, Bride's color is the mark of racial purity, and his and his wife's color indicate the stain of racial tampering.

Sweetness's revulsion at her daughter's color leads her to attempt to smother the baby, but she finds herself incapable of completing the act. Rather, she physically and emotionally distances herself from her offspring, going so far as to ask to be called "Sweetness" instead of "Mama." Sweetness attempts to justify her actions as a protective mechanism, but her disgust with her daughter's skin is evident: "[N]ursing her was like having a pickaninny sucking my teat. I went to bottle-feeding soon as I got home" (5). Morrison has interrogated the internal color line before, but Sweetness's claim clarifies that more is at stake than a greater degree of respect from white people and ease in negotiating social situations. "But how else can we hold on to a little dignity?" (4) Sweetness asks. For her, refusing the knowledge of her ancestral connection to slavery, to the "non-Human," is vital if she is to retain her sense of being. Mae Henderson has spoken of "the wounding at the 'primal scene' of slavery [which] becomes imprinted on black bodies, internalized in the black psyche, and passed down to subsequent generations" (224). Sweetness and Bride both suffer from such wounding. To maintain her sense of her *own* personhood, her *interiority*, which she predicates upon her light skin, Sweetness deprives Bride of hers, seeing only her child's surface and refusing to acknowledge the child's desire for a connection with her mother. Because Sweetness prides herself on her "high yellow" skin, she can scarcely bring herself to touch, much less love, her daughter. Bride recalls, "Distaste was all over her face when I was little and she had to bathe me. [...] I used to pray she would slap my face or spank me just to feel her touch. I made little mistakes deliberately, but she had ways to punish me without touching the skin she hated" (31). Sweetness's abhorrence of her child's surface eradicates any sense that Bride is more than simply skin, leaving the child to "[equate] herself with her appearance" (Wyatt 17). Judith Butler's argument that sexed identity is formed for some and foreclosed for others might apply here racially as well. She maintains that the creation of a subject "requires the simultaneous production of a domain of abject beings, those who are not yet 'subjects,' but who form the constitutive outside to the domain of the subject. The abject designates here precisely those 'unlivable' and 'uninhabitable' zones of social life which are nevertheless densely populated by those who do not enjoy the status of the subject." She goes on to point out that the subject will come to understand itself only through resisting that which it has cast off as abject. Therefore, "the subject is constituted through the force of exclusion and abjection, one which produced a constitutive outside to the subject, an abjected outside, which is, after all, 'inside' the subject as its own founding repudiation" (3). Lucille Fultz maintains that "Morrison explodes myths about difference by refiguring aesthetics in what has traditionally been deemed ugly, unnatural, freakish—all the negative baggage we bring to physical difference. It must be noted, however, that such notions of difference are generally measured against some standard of normativity—color, phenotypic features, presence or absence and arrangement of certain body parts" (18–19). Little Lula Ann Bridewell must come to a sense of identity in the face of the abjection she has experienced due to the perception of her mother and her community that her skin color is abnormal, even monstrous.

While Butler appears to suggest that the process she describes is inescapable in the developmental process and is that which demands of subjects the rejection of the abjected outside, in Bride's case, the abjected outside is her actual skin and therefore cannot be repudiated.

Bride's strategy initially suggests a claiming of agency and a refusal of her mother's renunciation. Abandoning her given name, she distances herself from any familial connectedness, both psychologically and geographically, since she escapes to Los Angeles, where, with the help of a "'total person' designer" (33), she recreates herself as the antithesis of what she had earlier been perceived to be. Whereas her mother had regarded her color as "terrible," and her early jobs were those out of the public eye, after she is remade (her term), her color becomes an asset, not a liability. She dresses only in white and wears no makeup; given her height and her slimness, as well as her haunting blue eyes, she relates, "Everywhere I went I got double takes but not like the faintly disgusted ones I used to get as a kid. These were adoring looks, stunned but hungry" (34). However, Bride carries within herself a racialized sense of abjection that she continually must reject. Hence, she fires her maid because "I could no longer stand the sight of her—fat, with cantaloupe breasts and watermelon behind" (57). Bride recasts the "uninhabitable" not as color, which she cannot escape yet can rescript, but rather as physicality itself, which, because she is young and wealthy enough to have sufficient leisure time to engage a trainer, she can regulate for the time being.

She begins by jettisoning her birth name—Lula Ann Bridewell—choosing to rename herself as simply Bride. Within this fiction, her act erases the Name-of-the-Father, which would seemingly free her from what Butler calls "nominal zones of phallic control" (153). According to Lacan, the Name-of-the-Father, sometimes simply referred to as the Father's "No," or even more simply, Law, interjects itself between the mother and the child, disrupting the child's desire for primal unity. However, in Bride's case—or rather, in Lula Ann's case—there is no father to claim the mother for himself; rather, the mother herself is repulsed by the child and refuses any form of intimacy with her. Whereas Lacan would argue that all children come into being as subjects when they recognize the mother's desire for something other than themselves, Bride has to confront the reality that her mother does not desire her at all. Fultz states, "While the women in Morrison's fiction endure and sometimes transcend different kinds of pain, the sources of their pain are often similar: pain accumulates to them from their multiple subject positions and often results from poverty and abandonments, or from parental, spousal, communal, and institutional abuse" (50). However, Lacan maintains that children "are concerned to secure (themselves) a place, to try to be the object of their parents' desire" (Fink 54). Presumably, in a more typical household, the child is sometimes successful in achieving such a place; Bride is not, until, by virtue of a lie that results in another woman's imprisonment, she briefly enjoys her mother's attention and affection. However, Sweetness's acceptance of her child is short-lived; hence, Bride is effectively orphaned,[2] even though she has living parents.

Furthermore, to become a subject, interpellation must occur, "interpellation" being Althusser's term for the process by which a person is "hailed" and subsequently responds, taking on the qualities associated with the "name" one is called (for example, "girl," "white," "poor"), and thus entering the social order. In Bride's case, Sweetness refuses to "hail" her child as "daughter," which leaves the girl ungrounded. One might argue she is first interpellated when, caught observing her landlord raping a little boy, the man refers to her as "nigger cunt," words she had never heard before and did not comprehend, although "the hate and revulsion in them didn't need definitions" (56). Her girlhood is marked by recurring racial slurs resulting from her color, "the name-calling [. . .] like poison, like lethal viruses through [her] veins, with no antibiotic available" (57). In choosing to rename herself, Bride is rejecting the earlier interpellation and using her color against those who had formerly antagonized her. She admits, "[F]orcing those tormentors—the real ones and others like them—to drool with envy when they see me is more than payback. It's glory" (57), an emotional stance that is completely understandable. Essentially, "Bride" is a fiction the young woman creates as an acceptable substitute for Lula Ann, whom she finds too repellant to inhabit. However, in erasing the existence of the girl child, Bride sets into motion a series of erasures that threatens to eradicate her. Furthermore, the name she chooses, "Bride," places her in a liminal space, neither daughter nor wife, unclaimed for the moment by either father or husband, and, as such, bearing the name of neither.

In refusing the Name-of-the-Father, of Law, and refusing interpellation, Bride is barred from entering what Lacan calls the symbolic order, the social order, predicated upon language, in which we exist as subjects. In the Lacanian scheme, infants at some point (usually between six and eighteen months) enter what he calls the mirror stage (or the imaginary order), in which the child sees its image in a mirror and perceives itself as identical with its image, which it construes as whole, unified, and possessed of agency (*Ecrits*, 1–4). Once the child acquires language (and is interpellated), it enters the symbolic order, where it both becomes a subject and becomes subjected to society's mores. Bride remains fixed in the mirror stage, the stage of misrecognition, mistakenly perceiving herself as a unified whole with full agency, requiring no one else, completely depending upon herself.[3] Bride misidentifies her entire self with her surface, as what she sees in the mirror; hence, she relates scenes from her own life to films or photographs she has seen, effectively reducing human complexity to generated image, rendering her depth impermeable, available neither to herself nor to anyone else. She comments that of the men she dated, "none [were] interested in what I thought, just what I looked like" (37) but admits that she had created "a shield that protected her from any overly intense feeling, be it rage, embarrassment, or love" (79). However, having given herself over purely to image, to a visual construction of a woman, effectively Bride has substituted representation for that which is represented, relying on media constructions to inform her understanding of lived experience. She compares her relationship with Booker to "double-page spreads in fashion magazines [. . .] with couples standing half naked in surf, [. . .] their sexuality like lightning and the sky going dark to show off the shine of their skin" (9), and decides her own relationship doesn't measure up. Again, when she sees an older couple holding hands, she envisions their "[s]teps matching, looking straight ahead like people called to a spaceship where a door will slide open and a tongue of red carpet rolls out. They will ascend, hand in hand, into the arms of a benevolent Presence. They will hear music so beautiful it will bring you to tears" (39). Of course, her cinematic vision of the couple's ascension to heaven reveals much about her own desires, but that she cannot view the two without scripting a scene for them indicates her obsession with image and suggests how her sense of reality is predicated upon the gaze and upon herself as being gazed upon, her surface the only existing certainty. Laura Mulvey, in her iconic essay "Visual Pleasure and Narrative Cinema," includes a discussion of the Lacanian Mirror Stage as it relates to film, pointing out that the experience of being so absorbed in a film that the world outside the screen vanishes is "nostalgically reminiscent" of the child's first perception of itself in a mirror (441). However, for Mulvey (and also for Lacan), recognition differs depending on the gender of the child who is looking into the mirror or watching the film.[4] Mulvey maintains, "In their traditional exhibitionist role women are simultaneously looked at and displayed, with their appearance coded for strong visual and erotic impact so that they can be said to connote to-be-looked-at-ness" (442). Bride predicates her entire existence on her surface, transforming herself into an object to be looked at. Her stunning beauty, once the "whole person designer" is finished with her, enables that transformation.

Bride capitalizes on her looks and launches a cosmetic line for women of all colors; her choice of a career is telling. Bride achieves fame and fortune not only by reconstructing herself as an icon but also by promoting products that enable women to transform and enhance their surface, their faces. However, devoid of a foundational self, she bases her identity purely on surface, incapable of perceiving interiority in herself or in others. She completely misreads the motives of her colleague Brooklyn (herself equally obsessed with image—blond with dreadlocks), whom she trusts as a close friend, even though Brooklyn reveals her disdain for Bride and even attempts to seduce Booker. Additionally, although she enjoys her relationship with Booker, Bride is content to allow that relationship to remain purely superficial, the result being that she knows nothing of Booker's life, his passions, even what he does while she works. She relishes their sexual relationship but overlooks the absence of any real intimacy between them. She admits that "what was important in our relationship, other than our lovemaking [was] his complete understanding of me" (61), unaware that when she spoke, Booker was not actually listening to her words but was admiring her beauty. When he leaves her, Bride assuages her longing for him by running his shaving brush over the surface of her skin. While she admits the sensation is not quite the same as sex with him, she acknowledges that her actions allow her to "imagine without grief times when I was made fun of and hurt" (35), revealing the purpose he served in her life—compensation for childhood lack.[5] Fultz states,

> At the core of Morrison's fiction is the issue of how to construct race as a discursive subject and simultaneously create individual subjectivities and the possibilities for intersubjective relations. [...] Achieving intersubjective relations, however, is often difficult because of real and perceived barriers. Such barriers include physical manifestations of difference such as "racial" features. When Morrison asserts that once race enters her texts, even as she attempts to reduce its relevance or situate it at the margins while foregrounding different categories of identity, she is, nevertheless, aware that race is such a powerful image that it is certain to mobilize expectations. (21)

In the case of Bride's relationship with Booker, the maternal revulsion which scarred the girl, a revulsion based on the child's surface, her skin, drives the adult woman's decision to refuse genuine intimacy. While it would seem that race would be a nonissue for Booker and Bride, Bride's scalding memories of the rejection she faced, specifically from other African Americans, specifically because of her color, allow insight into why she trusts people such as Brooklyn, who is white, more than she does Booker. Fultz points out, "In constructing the interiority of difference within the African American community, Morrison challenges the prevailing perception that white society must bear primary responsibility for African Americans' suffering, and she urges African Americans to consider their own complicity in and contribution to the suffering within the black community" (48). While communal rejection of Bride may have stemmed from preferential treatment given light-skinned blacks by white people, the members of the community have chosen to adopt those white values when they shun Bride.

Butler maintains that "[t]o prescribe an exclusive identification for a multiply constituted subject, as every subject is, is to enforce a reduction and a paralysis" (116). Bride, in choosing to exist purely as image, must foreclose memory, emotion, anxiety—the psychological compendium that would constitute a complete subject-position. Butler points out that all "subject-positions are produced in and through a logic of repudiation and abjection," but Morrison portrays Bride as having calculatingly chosen what to repudiate rather than to allow the process to happen more gradually and largely unconsciously, as it does for most humans as they undergo socialization. Butler continues, "The insistence on coherent identity [...] produces its coherence at the cost of its own complexity," and the Bride we meet in the early pages of the novel is certainly not complex, but rather shallow, mere surface, since to allow herself to expose her interiority would be to rupture her iconic status. While *on the surface*, Bride appears to have achieved not merely financial stability but also career fulfillment as well as adulation from all who see her, she does so only by refusing to incorporate her past into her current identity; as a result, she exists as image or icon, not as a more complexly realized subject. Morrison's strategic employment of a character who would appear to have succeeded in achieving the "American dream," a character many would envy and wish to emulate, is a bold move in that it challenges much contemporary understanding of what constitutes happiness. For all her creature comforts, Bride is not happy.

Bride's disquietude stems from an incident in her childhood when she achieves a degree of mother-love as well as celebrity after she scapegoats an innocent teacher accused of sexual molestation. Having witnessed, without completely understanding, their landlord raping a little boy, Bride is ordered by her mother to keep silent about what she has seen. When a public scandal ensues over teachers who may or may not have molested children, Bride gives the damning testimony that sends the young, innocent, female teacher to prison. In this instance, we see again her refusal of the Law of the Father, which demands honest testimony in a court of law. But in Bride's case, the lie she tells brings her rewards in the form of touch from the mother, her ongoing desire, and acceptance from the community that had previously been dismayed by her skin color. Hence, Bride comes to believe she can play by her own rules, which, to a large degree, she does. She makes her own place in the world as neither daughter nor wife nor mother, and she achieves immense financial success in the world of business, in spite of the multiple "fathers" that reign in that sphere.[6]

Given Bride's apparent callousness toward others, her desire to "rescue" Sofia, the young teacher falsely implicated, strikes the reader as incongruous. However, returning to my earlier discussion of abjection and the uninhabitable, one might argue that Bride identifies with Sofia in that both have been perceived as less than human—Bride because of her color, and Sofia because she is identified as a pedophile. Therefore, when Sofia is released from prison, Bride attempts to provide her with a new life: money, a plane ticket, and, of course, cosmetics. Having remade herself in a new setting with so little effort, Bride believes others can do so as well.

Intriguingly, though, the crime Bride actually observed, as well as the one for which she inculpates Sofia, calls attention to the skin: interior dynamic. Attracted by the appearance (skin) of the child, the pedophile penetrates the surface, causing lifelong trauma for the little boy. Whereas Bride's trauma is caused by the absence of touch, many of the other children in the novel (the boy being raped, Brooklyn as a girl, Rain, Adam) suffer from the violence of touch, a rupturing of surface. However, in all the cases, the perception of the skin drives the pain that the subjects will carry forever in their depth, that will mark them internally. While Morrison's concern for the abuse children suffer is very evident here, and turning the abuse into a metaphor for race might appear to diminish the significance of the crimes committed against these children, the fact remains that a parallel with the functioning of race in society is defensible. In both cases, the surface/skin results in treatment that impairs the depth/psyche.

Within the realm of fiction, however, healing and transformation can sometimes occur, as it does here. In the case of Bride, her desire to make amends for her childhood crime begins that process. However, she is stunned when her attempts to provide Sofia with a new identity are rejected; rather than showing gratitude, Sofia responds with violence and beats Bride senseless. Although Bride is obviously wounded—"[her] mouth looks as though it's stuffed with raw liver; the whole side of [her] face is scraped of skin; [her] right eye is a mushroom" (21)—she will not report the assault to the police for fear she will be photographed looking so unlike her usual stunning self. Intriguingly, though, Bride connects her abandonment by Booker with her assault by Sofia, seeing both events as having "erased" her (38). The term through which she accesses the incidents suggests, again, how she predicates her identity purely upon surface. Erasure removes a layer that has been applied to a surface beneath it. Bride's narrative, however, indicates that the actions of Booker and Sofia have obliterated the young woman's entirety; she does not appear to recognize a depth beneath the image she projects. However, the actual tearing of her flesh and the abrading of the black skin that was the source of her originary trauma allows what is beneath to be revealed, functioning as a metaphor for the beginning of her integration of self, a fusion of the surface:depth pseudo-binary.

Given that Bride's obsession with surface and skin, and her repression of emotion and reflection, began in childhood, psychologically she must return to that site if she is to become whole. Butler claims, "Bodies only become whole, i.e., totalities, by the idealizing and totalizing specular image which is sustained through time by the sexually marked name. To have a name is to be positioned within the Symbolic, the idealized domain of kinship" (72). Given that Bride has not entered the Symbolic, that she has no sexually marked name, her body—in this case—her literal flesh, no longer maintains its integrity. Bride's body, the surface on which she has sculpted herself as an aesthetic object, begins reverting to childhood: first her pubic hair, then the holes in her ears and her breasts disappear, and finally her menses halt. Butler claims, "There must be a body trembling before the law, a body whose fear can be compelled by the law, a law that produced the trembling body prepared for its inscription" (65). Prior to this time, Bride's body might be said to be immaterial, a flat surface, and therefore outside of the law. Even when Sofia ferociously beats her, Bride does not focus on her pain as much as on her image, hence her refusal to report the crime. Therefore, Bride must return to the site of her refusal of the Law of the Father, the time of her denial of that law, a move imposed on her by her bodily transformation.

Once she physically returns to girlhood, Bride abandons her posh but empty life to begin what from a Jungian perspective one might consider a night journey to self-actualization. Recognizing both that she may have perhaps actually loved Booker and that she has no clue about his life apart from her, Bride chooses to pay a bill that has arrived in the mail for him in an attempt to perhaps locate him. One might argue that, metaphorically, her act indicates another attempt to atone, to pay, as it were, for her previous mistakes, even though her first such attempt left her battered. Her task requires her to remove herself geographically from the elegance with which she has surrounded herself—a gorgeous condo, posh restaurants, elite clubs—and to begin to acknowledge life that is not aesthetic, not a simulacrum of desire, but one that grows out of poverty and a will to survive. I am most definitely not suggesting that the lives of the poor are somehow more authentic than other lives; rather, I am claiming that Bride has chosen to isolate herself in a world predicated purely on image. She reflects, "There were music shops in unthreatening neighborhoods" (73), which is obviously true, and her anxieties as an attractive woman in such a threatening neighborhood are fathomable, but she focuses on the "tattooed men and young girls dressed like ghouls" (73), who in all likelihood pose no danger to her but rather offend her visual sensibilities in their display of surface.

Just as Bride's body has taken her back to childhood, her travel takes her historically back in time, to worlds she has never imagined, worlds far removed from the pages of the glossy magazines that constitute her only reading material. Bride's journey to selfhood involves a quite literal journey, in her automobile, a Jaguar, which she crashes into "what must have been the world's first and biggest tree" (82); she is no longer in a world she recognizes. Morrison's nod toward the origins of life on the planet points to Africa, where we understand human life to have begun. Bride therefore has returned to her racial foundation, which she has refused to confront, thereby preventing her from constructing an identity of herself grounded in history, in depth, rather than on merely surface. She is rescued by a white, middle-aged hippie couple, living off the grid in a house with no running water or bathroom. Effectively, Bride moves back in time forty or fifty years, when a life such as theirs was not atypical for many Americans but is, of course, horrifying to the privileged Bride. Even as the woman into whose home she is taken provides clothes for her and offers her breakfast, Bride notices only her "unfashionable hips" (86). However, Bride is flummoxed by the couple's seeming obliviousness to her beauty and her mission as well as by their kindness: "They hadn't asked her where she was from or where she was going. They simply tended her, fed her, arranged for her car to be towed for repair. It was too hard, too strange for her to understand the kind of care they offered—free, without judgment" (90). Having embraced a world driven by economics, where every act or gesture can be recorded as either an asset or a liability, wherein one is continually evaluating gains and losses and determining behavior based on outcomes, Bride must confront a situation in which such a value system does not obtain, one in which earlier understandings of the obligations of hospitality are taken seriously. In this case, however, Bride might also be said to return to her infancy to start over, with Steve and Evelyn acting as the parents the child Lula Ann needed. Steve rescues her from the trapped car (a kind of birth) and carries her in his arms, while Evelyn bathes and feeds her as though she is an infant—which is essentially how she acts, "crying every minute, petulant, childish and unwilling to help herself or accept aid gracefully from others" (90). Since Bride is fairly incapable of movement, and since their home is so small, Bride sleeps on the couch, which, in the "deep darkness at night," makes Bride feel as though she is in a coffin. The death-rebirth imagery is complete here. Her constructed self is destroyed when the car crashes, and in the process of recovery, Bride's all-white wardrobe is replaced by flannel shirts and a pair of girls' jeans. Bride gradually overcomes her initial revulsion at the condition of the couple's home and to Steve and Evelyn's adopted (stolen) daughter, Rain, who functions as a parallel to the child Lula Ann. Rain is "bone-white," with intensely green eyes, and is usually in the company of her pet, a completely black kitten. As a negative of the blue-black Bride who dresses only in white, Rain survived a childhood far more devastating than

Bride did; Rain's mother prostituted out her daughter and then threw the six-year-old out when she bit the man on whom she was expected to perform fellatio. Rain teaches Bride all the street knowledge she gained before Steve and Evelyn rescued her—how to find safe spaces to sleep, how to find food, how to avoid the police, etc. Rain's response to her formerly brutal life is the beginning of the end of Bride's self-absorption: "Listening to the tough little girl who wasted no time on self-pity, she felt a companionship that was surprisingly free of envy. Like the closeness of schoolgirls" (103). Wyatt argues that "the extreme maternal rejection encountered by Rain cuts through Bride's habitual self-absorption. She experiences fellow feeling for another's suffering" (184), a sensation hitherto unexperienced by her. The age difference that initially would appear to keep the two from any real connection is leveled as Bride's body grows younger and smaller; however, in this reborn life, Bride fills in a gap missing in her development—a true friend. When a racist redneck attacks Rain, Bride acts selflessly for perhaps the first time ever; she throws out an arm to save Rain from birdshot, her hand and arm bloodied in the process. Once again, the rupturing of her skin becomes emblematic of her process of recovery, of integrating surface and depth. This time, however, she chooses to make herself vulnerable; Rain claims Bride saved her life "without even thinking about it" (106). By this time, Bride has opened herself to "new capacities that enable her to begin the move away from the identity of an abused child" (Wyatt 186) and to tentatively adopt a form of maternal sensitivity.

Once she is recovered, Bride continues her search for Booker; she leaves behind Booker's shaving brush, her sexual surrogate for him, suggesting that she is now willing to entertain the possibility that a relationship, a true intimacy, demands probing deep, which she is now capable of doing. Having experienced a rupture of her beautiful skin, her depth has been exposed and brought to the light, which will begin her healing process. Morrison's wicked humor reveals itself in a delicious parallel to Bride's transformation; her Jaguar, once the visual representation of her status, has been equally ruptured, now sporting a door of a color different from the rest of the vehicle. Additionally, just as Bride's body has transformed into the body of a child, her Jaguar has been replaced by Rain's black kitten, an authentic cat instead of a representation of a cat. As she proceeds further into the countryside, she encounters poverty that she cannot understand: the houses appear to be "worn boxes hiding shiftless residents" (141) and she speculates, "It's one thing for onetime hippies to live their anticapitalist ideals near the edge of a seldom-traveled country road. [...] But what about regular plain folks who were born in these places and never left?" (141). Bride cannot imaginatively enter the lives of others, whether those others find aesthetic pleasure in country living, whether they choose to live where they have roots, or whether they simply are too poor to live elsewhere. When Bride discovers the address she is seeking, she encounters Queen Olive, not the rival she had expected but "a heavyset red-headed woman" who is Booker's aunt but functions as a primal great mother, having had "lots" of children with her seven husbands who span the globe. Queen's initial assessment, "You look like something a raccoon found and refused to eat" (144), stuns Bride, who has come to expect adoration for her appearance. Queen's words return the young women to the time "she was the ugly, too-black little girl in her mother's house" (144), a return necessary for Bride to begin again, to move to maturity with a self in tow. Through Queen, Bride encounters an alternate aesthetic, as well as another return to racial origins; in the older woman's orderly home, Bride discovers homemade "[c]urtains, slipcovers, cushions, [and] embroidered napkins" (145). These lovely and elegant emblems of the woman's creative impulses manifest in ornamentation for her home; these aesthetic objects are not intended for display but rather fuse form and function in an art that unites surface with depth. Like a primal mother/crone/witch, Queen feeds Bride wholesome, nourishing food, which Bride describes as "manna" (145); Bride has entered an alternate reality, a fairy tale where she is given both sustenance and the information she needs to complete her search both for Booker and for a self.[7] She learns of the murder of Booker's brother, which he had never once mentioned to her, and how his reaction has been to have that "death become his own life [...] his only life" (147). She also reads Booker's journal, which he had written about her. His insights into her persona are accurate: "Her imagination [...] cuts and scrapes the bone never touching the marrow where the dirty feeling is [...] for her permanent ignorance is so much better than the quick of life" (149). However, he is less astute when it comes to self-analysis. By now, however, Bride is transforming, as is evident in her seeing Olive simply as a "heavyset red-headed woman" (142); and later, after the woman is badly burned, Bride tends her with loving devotion, believing that after she recovers, she, Bride, and Booker can live together in "[a] big mobile home" (171), a consideration unfathomable to the earlier Bride.

Booker's past is profoundly different from Bride's. Raised in a large, loving family with parents who deeply connected with their children, his idyll is shattered when his adored older brother Adam is kidnapped and murdered by a pedophile. When the child's body is found, maggots and the elements have reduced it to a skeleton, pure interiority, eradicating skin and flesh to point at all human finality. While the other members of his family gradually pull themselves out of despair and find a way to keep on living, Booker shuts down emotionally. Only after he first sees Bride does he begin to reawaken to life. As he plays his trumpet in the rain

> what emerged was music he had never played before. [...] Booker had no words to describe his feelings. What he did know was that the rain-soaked air smelled like lilac when he played while remembering her. Streets with litter at their curbs appeared interesting, not filthy; bodegas, beauty shops, diners, thrift stores leaning against one another looked homey, downright friendly. Each time he imagined her eyes glittering toward him or her lips open in an inviting, reckless smile, he felt not just a swell of desire but also the disintegration of the haunt and gloom in which for years Adam's death had clouded him. (132)

However, once he actually meets Bride and enters into a somewhat long-term relationship with her, perhaps her shallowness or perhaps his reversion to a psychic position that is comfortable and enabling to him allows him to forget his experience in the rain. Rather, he "especially liked her lack of interest in his personal life" (133) and believes that her distance from her parents "meant that, like him, she was free of family ties. It was just the two of them" (134). Marc

C. Conner maintains, "The figure of the outcast, the exile, the preterite, dominates Morrison's fiction as it dominates modernity; she rightly perceives that the crisis of modernity is *homelessness*, in its most far-reaching sense" (20). Both Booker and Bride have rejected their homes and their families, choosing homelessness in the sense of a disconnectedness from their roots. While Bride has created a home of a sorts for herself, Booker appears to drift from woman to woman. His irrational belief that he and Bride can escape the greater social interaction required of all fully functioning adults denotes not merely his immaturity but a dangerous insularity. Booker's and Bride's inability or refusal to allow their relationship to develop into a true, rather than merely a sexual, intimacy results in Booker's running away in horror when he learns of Bride's intention to offer assistance to Sofia, whom he believes is a pedophile.

Whereas Bride's initial sense of identity is constituted purely by skin, by image, using the color her mother hated as an asset and a weapon (she claims, "I sold my elegant blackness to all those childhood ghosts and now they pay me for it" [57]), Booker refuses to acknowledge skin as having any cultural signification, relying on the scientific finding that race does not exist, that it is "just a color [. . .] not a flaw, nor a curse" (143). Bride perceives the logic in what he argues but understands that his words "had little to do with day-to-day experience" (143). Booker's understanding that race does not register scientifically does not change the fact that racism exists. However, Booker rejects surface, image, color, as having any consequence, reading slavery purely through its economic, rather than its personal, implications. He "suspected most real answers concerning slavery, lynching, forced labor, sharecropping, racism, Reconstruction, Jim Crow, prison labor, migration, civil rights, and black revolution movements were all about money" (110). When he finds a discipline that allows him to buttress his preconceptions with theory—the field of economics—he feels justified in claiming that "money shaped every single oppression in the world and created all the empires, nations, colonies with God and His enemies employed to reap, then veil, the riches" (111). While no rational person can deny the partial truth of Booker's standpoint, he chooses to detach himself from the knowledge of pure racial hatred based on skin color and refuses to recognize a shared humanity. Furthermore, the disingenuousness of his argument is evident in that it cannot explain his brother's violation and murder; the pedophile who killed Adam and the other boys was not by any means wealthy, nor did he discriminate in choosing his victims—"[c]learly an equal-opportunity killer" (118), in Booker's words. Hence, Booker "knows" but chooses not to acknowledge that some forms of oppression are not determined by economics, nor does race figure in every kind of oppression. Booker's view of racism is clean, if you will; once black people can achieve a degree of wealth, racism will disappear, he seems to believe. As a result he drifts, relying on his intellect to maintain his sense of superiority and disdain. Lauren Berlant points out how "disappointment can be channeled as though it were a judgment rather than a feeling, supporting the mytheme that the solitary and independent life of the brain precedes and is superior to the simple attachments of intimate proximity" (261). This is evident in Booker's self-described "riveting intellectual journey that policed his anger, caged it and explained everything about racism, poverty, and war. The political world was anathema; its activists, both retro and progressive, seemed wrongheaded and dreamy. The revolutionaries, armed or peaceful, had no notion of what should happen after they 'won.' Who would rule? The 'people'? Please" (122).

While Bride would eagerly abandon all memories of her childhood and the pain it carried, Booker is angry with his family for refusing him access to his. After Adam's death, Booker returns home to find that his sister Carole has moved into the bedroom he formerly shared with his brother and that she logically has redecorated it in a more feminine style. His fury drives a quarrel with his father that culminates in his leaving home forever. In his family's choice to continue with their lives, Booker perceives "the savage absence not only of Adam but of himself" (125). As a result, he essentially never grows up; he finishes degrees but seeks no position concomitant with them; he plays trumpet in a makeshift ensemble that plays on the street; he writes poetry and reads voraciously but is completely comfortable with relying on Bride to provide for him financially. She buys him clothes (which he often does not wear), provides him a home, takes him to clubs and restaurants, and provides a life that he seemingly can do without. He completely guards his interiority, never sharing either his thoughts or his writing with anyone, and he cavalierly ignores his surface, while he enjoys hers immensely, loving her look and her body but repelled, eventually, by what he finds beneath.

The act of physical penetration—first by a penis, and then by a knife—that destroyed Adam propels Booker to live purely within himself, coming out of his self-containment only to have sex without intimacy with Bride. After Adam's killer was arrested, it was discovered that he had tattooed the names of his victims on his skin. In response, Booker marks his own flesh with a rose tattoo to commemorate his having placed a rose on his brother's casket at the funeral. The tattoo inscribes both the acts of the serial killer and Booker's intimacy with Adam onto Booker's own flesh and effectively marks his own symbolic death, the absence he feels even in his family's home when he returns from college. He is mourning himself, his own stasis, through the emblem. Like Adam, he no longer matures in any meaningful way, growing intellectually but to no end, his life even more meaningless than Bride's simulacrum of existence.

Significantly, what jars Booker out of his somnolence is Bride's interaction with Sofia. The inability of both main characters to achieve integrated identity pivots around the image of the pedophile, the transgressor who marks both surface and depth through his or her degrading acts. In her discussion of black masculinity, Patricia Hill Collins argues that some male bodies are seen as more "authentically Black that those of middle-and-upper middle class African American men," and goes on to discuss how the stereotypes of the gangster and the player render other African American men insecure in their own masculinity (152). While I would maintain that her assessment is somewhat reductionist, it strikes me as particularly irrelevant in a discussion of Booker. Like all men, Booker must confront the threat of castration; however, in his case, that threat had been actualized on the body of his brother, whose murderer collected the penises of the boys he raped and killed. The moment Booker grasps what has happened to Adam is critical in his (lack of) development. Having experienced vicariously the greatest anxiety a boy child can imagine, he has no more fears, but he is frozen in his radical freedom, which removes him from the familial and the societal, severing all connections. Butler maintains that the "symbolic position that marks a sex as masculine is one through which the masculine sex is said to 'have' the phallus; it is one that compels through the threat of punishment, that is, the threat of feminization, and imaginary, and, hence, inadequate identification" (101). However, Booker is freed from the threat of castration, since it has already happened, so feminization, in the sense of passivity, acquiescence, creates no anxiety for him. His masculinity is irrelevant to him because he has relinquished it. Rather than to symbolically kill the father to become the father, Booker leaves home, leaving his father's authority unchallenged but also stranding him in an infantile Oedipal situation, seeking out women who will provide for him—first Felicity, who takes him in when he is homeless, and later Bride. His relationship, such as it is, with Felicity ends when Booker attacks a man who is busy with a crack pipe and ignoring his crying toddler. Felicity's callous comment, "It wasn't your kid and it wasn't your business" (129), should not enable us to overlook Booker's complete identification with the crying child, hence his extreme reaction. Similarly, the high-minded young man can overlook his grandfather's "greed and criminality" (130) so as to accept an inheritance from the old man whom he had disdained. The money enables him to provide a home for himself and to play his music, not for money, which he regards as "pitiful," but for a "nonpaying, therefore uncritical, undemanding audience" (130). His refusal to secure paying gigs, with audiences who would expect more from him, provides more evidence of his passivity, since he declines any arena in which he is judged by other men. Bride then replaces Felicity as the symbolic mother who provides for all his needs, including sex, demanding nothing of him. Booker's tremendous intellect, his undergraduate experience, which begins with the cynicism the narrative refers to as "a young man's version of critical thinking" (121), quickly leads him to depression as "his classmates began to both bore and bother him, not only because they were predictable but also because they blocked serious inquiry" (121). However, Booker turns his intellectual acumen into no useful activity because he is incapable of any adult endeavor. Rather, he enjoys (when he is not irritated by) Bride's vapidity as well as her generosity in providing for him but demanding nothing of him in the way of an adult partnership. However, his ignorance of the fact that Bride had *falsely* accused Sofia, his belief that she is forgiving a pedophile, acts as an emotional trigger, returning him once again to the moment of Adam's death and dismemberment. He runs away but this time is pursued both by Bride, who demands an explanation for his behavior, and by Queen, whose very candid assessment of his self-delusion enables him to recognize Adam for what he has functioned as: the *objet a* for which all else becomes a substitute. Booker finally admits, "Had [Adam] lived, grown up to have flaws, human failings like deception, foolishness and ignorance, would he be so easy to adore or even be worthy of adoration? What kind of love is it that requires an angel and only an angel for its commitment?" (160). One might argue this is an epiphanic moment for Booker; he comes to realize that human love requires accepting the flaws in the beloved as well as recognizing the imperfections in the self. As a result, he is finally able to acknowledge his own irresponsibility and effectively grow up. He and Bride lovingly tend Queen after her severe burns, "work[ing] together like a true couple, thinking not of themselves, but of helping somebody else" (167). When Bride informs him that she is pregnant and that the baby is his, he responds, "No, it's ours" (174), indicating his desire to take on adult obligations. One wonders how consciously Morrison chose the name of the woman who drives the two main characters to self-actualization, since "Sofia" means "wisdom," which is what they acquire.

It is, however, facile to read the early Bride and Booker only as shallow and lacking in self-awareness. As Collins points out, "So much fear accompanies being African American—fear of being unloved, alone, disrespected, ignored, ridiculed, too visible, invisible, silenced or forgotten" (304). That fear is evident in Bride's insecurity and Booker's insularity. That they are able to finally communicate honestly with each other demonstrates their willingness to let go of their fear and to allow for growth. Collins maintains, "For African American women, men, and transgendered people, the dreams catalyzed within a context of oppression remain limited—oppression crowds out the possibilities of new, more liberatory dreams" (305). However, she adds, "For individuals, claiming new identities of race, gender, and sexuality, and seeing one another in honest and loving ways, reverses the process of dehumanization associated with oppression" (306). Bride's relinquishing of her self-created image of herself as an aesthetic object and Booker's ability to let go of the idealized image of his brother enable this reversal of the process of dehumanization.

If the novel were to end with the young lovers affirming their determination to be stellar parents, we might wonder if we were reading a Victorian novel. Even as it is, as Wyatt maintains, "[t]o a reader of Morrison's earlier novels, [this] resolution may seem too easy" (177). But Morrison leaves the ending open, to some degree. The last words of the text are given to Sweetness, who has just learned she is to become a grandmother and sarcastically remarks, "Good move, Lula Ann. If you think mothering is all cooing, booties and diapers you're in for a big shock. [...] You are about to find out what it takes, how the world is, how it works and how it changes when you are a parent" (178). Her words are no doubt true, but Booker and Bride will undertake the challenges of commitment and parenthood as adults who have tamed, if not slain, the dragons that tortured them during their extended childhood and adolescence. That is the best that anyone can ask of human beings.

Notes

1. The focus on intraracial bias predicated upon skin color is a major trope in Morrison's first novel, *The Bluest Eye*, as well as in *Paradise*, where she inverts expectations in creating a community of blue-black families who refuse connection with lighter-skinned African Americans.

2. The orphaned child is a recurring motif in Morrison's work, likely calling attention to the disruption in the African American family as a result of slavery and the concept of the child as property. However, irresponsible or cruel parents also populate these novels, with resulting trauma to the children that carries over into their adulthood. Intriguingly, though, even though Bride's childhood is nightmarish and certainly loveless, as Jean Wyatt points out, "the narration of *God Help the Child* betrays an impatience with the residues of trauma that hold back its characters from loving anew" (171).

3. As I argue in my "Across Distances without Recognition: Misrecognition in Toni Morrison's *A Mercy*," Morrison savages her characters Jacob and Rebekka for their belief that they can survive on their own, not needing a community. Her impatience with such insular thinking is palpable in that novel, but it recurs here as well. But Pecola's madness at the end of *The Bluest Eye*, Violet's loss of identity after Joe's betrayal of her in *Jazz*, and Denver's desolation at her and Sethe's rejection by the community in *Beloved* are other obvious examples of her exploration of this theme.

4. Lacan refers to "Men" as [t]hose who, from a psychoanalytic perspective, are considered to be men—regardless of their biological/genetic makeup" (Fink 106) and makes the parallel claim for "Women." Essentially, even though the term "transgender" was not used extensively when Lacan wrote, it is evident that he does not equate a person's gender with that person's biological sex. I have chosen to use the word "gender" here because that is accurate, while "sex," with the complications of biology and genetics thrown in, is merely confusing in this context.

5. Lacan might consider the shaving brush to function as an *objet a* for Bride. Martin Jay defines the term as "the missing object that will seemingly satisfy the drive for plenitude. [...] At its most fundamental level, it is the phallus which the child [...] wishes to be in order to make up for the mother's alleged lack" (cited in Hawthorn 243). In the complicated relationship between Bride and Sweetness, the "lack" for which Bride grieves is the touch of the mother, which she never was able to possess. Booker's shaving brush, then, satisfies her need for gentle touch—not sexual touch per se, but the kind of touch a mother might employ with her infant.

6. As businesses go, however, the cosmetic industry is one in which women have fared quite well. The first American woman to become a millionaire in her own right, as opposed to inheriting family wealth, was Madame Walker, an African American woman who developed a line of cosmetics.

7. To read Queen simply as a mechanism driving Booker and Bride to adulthood demands overlooking her own story and her own pain. If Bride's color marks her as a throw-back to the early days of slavery, Queen also functions as an embodiment of the enslaved mother. We are told that she has had seven "husbands" who have snatched her children from her and that she has had "no opportunity to raise a single child beyond the age of twelve" (159). This situation quite obviously parallels the experiences of slave mothers who were violated by their "owners," and whose children were therefore enslaved to their fathers.

Works Cited

Berlant, Lauren. "Two Girls, Fat and Thin." *Feminisms Redux: An Anthology of Literary Theory and Criticism*, edited by Robyn Warhol-Down and Diane Price Herndl. Rutgers UP, 2009, pp. 244–73.

Butler, Judith. *Bodies That Matter: On the Discursive Limits of "Sex."* Routledge, 1993.

Collins, Patricia Hill. *Black Sexual Politics: African Americans, Gender, and the New Racism*. Routledge, 2004.

Conner, Marc C. "Toni Morrison and the Fictions of Modernism." *Toni Morrison: Memory and Meaning*, edited by Adrienne Lanier Seward and Justine Tally. UP Mississippi, 2014, pp. 19–32.

Eudell, Demetrius L. "'Come On Kid, Let's Go Get the Thing': The Sociogenic Principle and the *Being* of Being Black/Human." *Black Knowledges/Black Struggles: Essays in Critical Epistemology*, edited by Jason R. Ambroise and Sabine Broeck. Liverpool UP, 2015, pp. 21–43.

Fink, Bruce. *The Lacanian Subject: Between Language and Jouissance*. Princeton UP, 1995.

Fultz, Lucille P. *Toni Morrison: Playing with Difference*. U of Illinois P, 2003.

Hawthorn, Jeremy. *A Glossary of Contemporary Literary Theory*. 4th ed. Arnold, 2000.

Henderson, Mae. *Speaking in Tongues and Dancing Diaspora: Black Women Writing and Performing*. Oxford UP, 2014.

Lacan, Jacques. *Ecrits: A Selection*. Translated by Alan Sheridan. Norton, 1982.

Morrison, Toni. *The Bluest Eye*. Washington Square Press, 1970.

———. *God Help the Child*. Alfred A. Knopf, 2015.

———. *Paradise*. Plume, 1999.

Mulvey, Laura. "Visual Pleasure and Narrative Cinema." *Feminisms: An Anthology of Literary Theory and Criticism*, rev. ed., edited by Robyn R. Warhol and Diane Price Herndl. Rutgers UP, 1971, pp. 438–48.

Spillers, Hortense J. "Interstices: A Small Drama of Words." *Pleasure and Danger: Exploring Female Sexuality*, edited by Carole S. Vance, Routledge, 1984, pp. 152–75.

Stave, Shirley A. "Across Distances without Recognition: Misrecognition in Toni Morrison's *A Mercy*." *Toni Morrison's A Mercy: Critical Approaches*, edited by Shirley A. Stave and Justine Tally. Cambridge Scholars, 2011, pp. 137–50.

Wyatt, Jean. *Love and Narrative Form in Toni Morrison's Later Novels*. U of Georgia P, 2017.

The Power of Witnessing: Confronting Trauma in *God Help the Child*

Evelyn Jaffe Schreiber

Toni Morrison's final novel, *God Help the Child*, illustrates the possibility of confronting trauma to claim a worthy self through a complex process of testimony. Both Bride and Booker, the novel's protagonists, reconstruct past traumas, first by encountering people who activate buried memories and then by telling their stories to each other in the holding space they create. Together, Bride and Booker retrieve their childhood traumas to gain agency and self-esteem by "bearing witness" to their representative African American testimonies. In this way, Morrison's novel becomes a symbolic holding space for African American trauma.

Indeed, trauma has become increasingly popular in African American literary studies (and perhaps feminist studies in general) for over a decade, with trauma studies providing necessary cultural insights. *God Help the Child* explicitly revolves around how Bride and Booker overcome early traumas to go forward together. But Morrison is interested in the traumas of all of the characters and narrators she presents in this novel. Different characters narrate alternating chapters, with a third-person narrator giving the reader other information as well. Everyone wrestles with traumatic demons and how to live at peace in the present world: Sweetness, the high yellow mother who gives birth to a "blue-black" child, Lula Ann (who renames herself Bride); Sofia Huxley, the schoolteacher sent to prison for abusing her young pupils; Brooklyn, the white coworker and close friend of Bride, who is jockeying for Bride's position, having escaped her uncle's child abuse and reinvented herself as a self-sufficient adult; Rain, the sexually abused runaway discarded by her mother and rescued from the streets by the hippie couple Evelyn and Steve; and Queen, Booker's aunt who lives alone after abandoning her children and splitting from seven "husbands." These damaged people, through their interactions with Bride and Booker, find a solace, comfort, or disdain that helps them articulate their *own* personal experiences and their attempts to move beyond them. Some of these individuals also serve to elicit testimony from Bride and Booker by stimulating repressed memory so that our protagonists "know" what is repressed in order to work through layers of suppressed trauma. The complicated components of testimony reveal the elements of African American trauma that Bride and Booker must examine.

Art Blank categorizes extreme trauma events as "sudden and unnatural death," "war including terrorism," "assaults including rape," and "sexual or physical abuse *or* extreme neglect or abandonment in childhood" ("One" 1). Such trauma causes one to be "shattered, [and] one struggles to put together the pieces, so to speak, of the psyche, and to balance that need to reconstitute oneself with the capacity to take in the experience. [. . .] Recovery from posttraumatic effects, or from survivor conflicts, cannot really occur until that traumatized self is reintegrated" (Lifton 11). Thus, catastrophic trauma produces a disintegrated self, but Dori Laub's work with Holocaust survivors suggests that a fragmented personality can be rebuilt with the help of "testimony" to an "external listener" (50). The survivors Laub worked with needed "a totally present listener who creates the holding space for them. [. . .] Testimony is the healing of the wound by shaping and giving shape to an experience that's fragmented, a healing way of pulling fragments together" (48). It is important for this listener to be "from outside to help create an internal audience" (49). Laub found that people who were not encouraged by family or friends were "not assisted in beginning that process of transmitting, and then they atrophied. And the ego strength and the ability to verbalize and to symbolize atrophied" (49–50). It is quite destructive "when the imperative to tell is not met by a responsive audience" (50). A traumatized person feels "lack of support, of help, of comfort [of] being utterly left alone with the experience and having no one listening" (Van der Hart

202). "The person bearing witness needs to be responsive, exhibiting emotional resonance" in order for healing to take place (204–5).

This ability of trauma survivors to rebuild identity through testimony connects to Jacques Lacan's theory of subjectivity, where the fragmented self begins at birth, in a state Lacan calls the "Real" (*Seminar* 54). Unification of the self occurs in Lacan's "mirror stage," where a subject sees a perfect imaginary self reflected back. However, social and cultural forces outside the self destroy this sense of imaginary wholenesss, leaving one with a sense of lack (*Écrits* 2–4). In a culture that values whiteness, as Kaja Silverman writes, "only certain subjects have access to a flattering image of self, and [...] others have imposed upon them an image so deidealizing that no one would willingly identify with it" (29). This racial self-hatred, according to bell hooks, complicates the process of establishing black identity in white culture (33). Lacan's gaze of the white Other and one's own lack in its presence perpetuates fragmentation, fear, and trauma for black characters.

However, Lacan suggests that with an internalized knowledge of cultural erasure, people can enact change by moving from a socially constructed object to a subject with agency. Laub's internal listener to whom the survivor can testify is important for the movement into Lacan's subject position. As Laub claims, "the formation of narrative [needed for subjectivity] only happens within an internal dialogue. And a listener temporarily takes the place of that internal other, that addressee" (48). Gaining a sense of self depends on the collaborative interaction with an attentive, empathetic outsider.

In Morrison's novel, Bride and Booker develop into integrated subjects as their internal listeners take shape. By the novel's close, they can Testify, what Geneva Smitherman calls "verbal witness to the efficacy, truth, and power of some experience that all blacks shared" (58). Yvonne Atkinson describes how in "the oral tradition of Black English, Witness and Testify go hand in hand: one who Witnesses has an obligation to Testify. To Witness is to affirm, attest, certify, validate, and observe" (23). Further,

> Witness/Testify is a shared collective memory, a cultural ritual that promotes solidarity and cohesion, creating a living archive of African

American culture. Witnessing is shared experience, emotional, physical, communal, historical—it is social empathy. Testifying articulates and validates the shared experience through gesture, sign, symbol, or verbal expression. (23)

This idea of community testimony connects specifically to African American culture through three avenues of shared experience: the church, music, and community suffering.

The church, central to black lives, provides a space for the personal to interweave with the communal. Susan Hubert suggests that the "importance of the individual's relationship to the community has been emphasized throughout the history of African-American Christianity, in part because of the influence of African religions" (45). Further, in the "context of the African-American church, the primary narrative of life-in-community is the testimony. Testimony strengthens an individual's faith as well as the faith of the community" (Hubert 46). Even in pre-Revolutionary times in New England, African American testimony in Congregational churches revealed authentic black lives so as to reverse white racial stereotypes. One of the few handwritten accounts by Cuffee Wright, servant to Reverend Conant of Middleboro Church, conveyed his experiences as an enslaved black man while thoughtfully testifying before New Englanders in their own idiom. Churchgoers widely understood that African Americans possessed souls and were capable of spiritual equality, but among the more perspicacious of Middleboro's townspeople, Cuffee's penetrating relation must have stood as a challenge to New England's prevailing eighteenth-century racial assumptions (Cooper cited in Boles 308).

Such personal testimony to compassionate listeners strengthens black community life. Churchgoing blacks, according to J-Glenn Murray, "want to hear and experience survival both personal and communal, societal justice, deliverance, advancement, prosperity, and well-being in Christ's saving activity" (86). Personal and community salvation establishes the church as central to African American life.

Music provides another source of community healing. As "a model of testimony, black music not only affects the individual but also implicates a community, and the collective facets of this form of testimony are specific to the African American community" (Visvis 266). This musical testimony through "black music [...] brings latent memories to the fore, integrating dissociated recollections into consciousness" (Visvis 258). Personal memories mingle with collective ones as music verbalizes trauma. Burton Peretti discusses "the intimate relationship between jazz music and oral testimony. This relationship is rooted in African American cultural traditions" (583). Musicians develop "codes and methods similar to those that have long aided black survival and success. Music is part of a healthy expressive continuum that also includes language, body movement, dress, and other behavior. [...] Oral performance lies at the center of those crucially important forms of African American expression" (Peretti 594). In *God Help the Child*, grieving for his brother and lacking both words to express and someone to share his feelings, Booker finds comfort in playing his trumpet, whether alone or with other musicians.

Another avenue for black testimony comes through legal venues connected to court testimony or written legal documents. People who documented on record their physical and psychological abuse in white culture received agency from this process. Kidada Williams describes how "[t]estifying about racial violence was a crucial factor in African Americans' individual recovery and their collective resistance to white supremacy because whenever victims related their experiences of this violence, they created witnesses to their trauma" (5). Public testimonies on record provided a resistance that produced a "collective black body" out of individual suffering (Williams 10). Other individual testimonies that formed a collective voice were petitions of slaves to buy their freedom and/or the freedom of their relatives: "Petition testimonies contain evidence of how slaves, slaveholders and free African-Americans experienced the legal process of manumission. Petition narratives also offer a uniquely personal perspective on manumission that is understandably absent from recorded manumission deeds" (Dorsey 547). These petitions reflect authentic slave voices to validate both personal and communal suffering through "important details about African-Americans' inner world [that] provide some depth to our often one-dimensional image of black life" (556). Such articulation contributes to a sense of subject status.

In a way similar to these petitions, memoirs written during the civil rights era present not only "firsthand accounts that provide insight into black women's subjective experiences of civil rights era events, but also [serve] as memory texts that illuminate the complex relationship between individual testimony and cultural memory" (Berg 85). According to Danielle McGuire, such testimony in regard to rape or other sexual abuse "exposed the bitter ironies of segregation and white supremacy" as well as "helped to reverse the shame and humiliation rape inflicts" (914). These written records help the individual victims who verbalize their trauma and provide an archive of communal shame and abuse. According to Akinyela's work on "narrative therapy," culturally specific collective stories help marginalized people "reclaim their own voices and speak their own special truths" and move toward "healing methods to [their] own communities that are received as familiar and authentic" (48). Verbalizing trauma in a supportive space connects individual affliction to communal pain. Bride and Booker generate a healing space for testimony about personal trauma connected to their lives in black communities.

Morrison begins and ends *God Help the Child* with the voice of Sweetness, the "high yellow" mother who rejects her dark-skinned child, Lula Ann. Sweetness articulates her own trauma that results from Lula Ann's problematic deep black color: "It's not my fault. So you can't blame me. [...] Something was wrong. Really wrong. She was so black she scared me. Midnight black, Sudanese black" (3). Sweetness explains that her grandmother had passed for white, underscoring the generational and cultural trauma caused by the stigma of racial othering. Sweetness elaborates that in a segregated culture, "the lighter, the better" (4). Her grandmother passed because "how else can we hold on to a little dignity? How else can you avoid being spit on in a drugstore [...]?" (4). Passing provided the liberty to try on clothes in stores and drink from a public water fountain. That the problem is a national one rather than a local one reverberates when Sweetness thinks, "[H]ow many white folks have Negro blood running and hiding in their veins?" (3). When Lula Ann's light-skinned parents see their new baby, her color is a mystery. "It broke our marriage to pieces," Sweetness claims, chagrined that her husband couldn't bring himself to touch the child. Sweetness even considers smothering the baby. As a single mother, she had to be strict, knowing how her daughter's "color is a cross she will always carry. But it's not my fault" (7).

Two chapters in, Sweetness resurfaces to try and make amends, to verbalize her own trauma that she has never told her daughter: "I wasn't a bad mother, you have to know that, but I may have done some hurtful things to my only child because I had to protect her. [...] All because of skin privileges" (43). Looking back, Sweetness realizes that "What you do to children matters. And they might never forget" (43). With this direct address, Morrison sets up the reader as the outside witness for Sweetness, calling on the reader to accept her testimony and address her trauma as well as the trauma she has heaped upon her daughter. Thus, the reader must grapple with the national problem of racial othering and the trauma that ensues for the black community. The prevalent American racial hatred toward blacks provides an overarching societal trauma that impacts negatively the development of an integrated self. Within black communities, a hierarchy of shades of color assigns rank, and this colorism ignites the trauma that Sweetness and Bride inherit.

Bride's journey takes her from a fragmented self to an integrated subject through her testimony that connects her to the historical and ongoing trauma of the African American community in order to claim her dignity as a black woman. In turn, Booker must be able to live with his brother's horrific mutilation and death rather than carry it as a burden that prohibits him from living his own life with integrity. For both protagonists, a shared recognition of a worthy self despite traumatic erasure can lead to recovery. Laub would attribute the healing process to the creation of an inside listener or self who believes the traumatic events occurred and that one has survived intact. Such an inside presence forms only through the assistance of an outside listener.

Interestingly, Morrison revisits in this work her first novel, *The Bluest Eye*, where Pecola's community brands her as ugly for her dark black skin and poverty. But unlike Pecola and her community members, who are all doomed to accept the hopeless weight of racial othering, Lula Ann reinvents herself as Bride, a cosmetics guru who shines as an exotic black beauty, dressing only in white to highlight her ebony skin. Through her testimony in the novel, Bride will move from receiving validation as someone else's creation to creating her own authentic self. In contrast to the bleak landscape of Morrison's first novel, *God Help the Child* suggests hope for claiming a lovable self. But the road is not easy.

Bride's early childhood traumas erupt to erase her self-esteem, which is fragile at best. Cut off from her mother, Bride inhabits a new identity in an attempt to escape her childhood distress. Craving her mother's love, the eight-year-old Lula Ann testified in court by pointing to a teacher accused of child abuse. Although she herself was not abused, her testimony, along with those of other girls, convicted Sofia Huxley. This lie produced the effect Lula Ann dreamed of:

> I glanced at Sweetness; she was smiling like I've never seen her smile before. [...] As we walked down the courthouse steps she held my hand, my hand. She never did that before and it surprised me as much as it pleased me because I always knew she didn't like touching me. I could tell. Distaste was all over her face when I was little and she had to bathe me. [...] I used to pray she would slap my face or spank me just to feel her touch. (31)

Bride's guilt for lying and sending the teacher to prison causes her to try to make amends fifteen years later when Sofia makes parole. But when Bride offers her cash and airline tickets to make up for time in prison and the loss of a teaching career, Sofia explodes with physical violence toward Bride: "How could she think cash would erase fifteen years of life as death?" (70). This eruption has its seeds in Sofia's *own* childhood trauma in a home of punishment, obedience, and silence, a pattern that her husband repeated. Her emotional release causes Sofia to realize that "freedom is never free. You have to fight for it. Work for it and make sure you are able to handle it" (70). As she cries for the first time, Sofia realizes that Bride has gifted her "the release of tears unshed for fifteen years. Now I am clean and able" (70). Her encounter with Bride, an empathetic listener, allows Sofia to verbalize the childhood pain dormant in her unconscious: "Beating her, kicking and punching her freed me up more than being paroled. I felt I was ripping blue-and white wallpaper, returning slaps and running the devil Mommy knew so well out of my life" (77). As a health companion now, when working to soothe her patients, Sofia claims, "[I]n my mind I am putting the black girl back together, healing her, thanking her. For the release" (77). The encounter with Bride provides Sofia with the space to verbalize her early trauma.

At the same time, during Sofia's beating, Bride "reverted to the Lula Ann who never fought back" and when it was over "like a whipped puppy [. . .] just crawled away afraid to even whimper" (32). Bride has not yet had Sofia's epiphany about the hard work needed for freedom. When Bride tells Booker about the episode, he deserts her, claiming she is "not the woman I want" (8). These words wound Bride, leaving her feeling "erased" (13): "I told him everything about myself; he confided nothing" (11). Later she realizes, "I left him his private life. I thought it showed how much I trusted him. [. . .] I shouldn't have—trusted him. [. . .] I spilled my heart to him; he told me nothing about himself. I talked, he listened" and then "he split [. . .] dumping me exactly as Sofia Huxley did" (61). Bride thought that "his complete understanding of [her]" was important in the relationship and confided to Booker alone about her childhood (61). After telling Booker about her past, she "felt curried, safe, owned" (56). But because there has been no dialogue, only a one-way flow of information, Booker rejects her, and Bride has difficulty processing why he leaves.

Trying to get a handle on her sense of erasure when Booker deserts her, Bride wonders, "Why am I still so sad?" (9) despite the attainment of the commercial success with the "YOU, Girl" cosmetics she owns—"the idea, the brand, the campaign" (11). Despite her reinvention, the traumatized self remains. Bride asks herself, "So why am I so miserable? [. . .] I've gotten over all of that and moved on" (53). Her misery remains because she needs to articulate buried trauma through testimony to a compassionate witness, which comes only with her final physical confrontation with Booker (mirroring Sofia's attack on Bride). The world without Booker is "shallow, cold, deliberately hostile. Like the atmosphere in her mother's house" (78). Bride's testimony of childhood fear and abandonment will free her at the novel's end. Physically and emotionally depleted, Bride thinks Brooklyn is "the one person she can trust. Completely" (22). Bride will arrive at a place where she no longer needs Brooklyn or the competitive world that Brooklyn covets. But although she is close with Bride, Brooklyn has survived through her street smarts and intuition, and even though she does not know the whole truth about Bride's actions, she instinctively knows that Bride is hiding information from her—about Sofia, Booker, Bride's mother. Having formed superficial conclusions about Booker, Brooklyn lacks real insight into his complicated identity, seeing him only as a conquest to steal from the ungrateful Bride. Having failed to seduce Booker, Brooklyn focuses on replacing Bride at work. In a variation of Bride's use of outer appearances that belie individual qualities, Brooklyn's blond dreadlocks play into the creation of a false self, a facade to appear exotic and attract black men. Brooklyn's assessment of Bride's "stupid" actions—her feeling abandoned by Booker, her guilt over Sofia, and her running off to find the "con man" Booker—give Brooklyn a sense of superiority (140). Having avoided her uncle's abuse by running away, Brooklyn has emerged as a strong, hardworking person and will take advantage of opportunities that materialize. Bride's actions, misunderstood by Brooklyn, nevertheless enable Brooklyn to articulate her own subjectivity.

Bride's path to self-analysis begins with a regression that began with her encounter with Sofia, thinking, "Something bad is happening to me. I feel like I'm melting away" (8). With her artful magic realism, Morrison reduces Bride to the "scared little black girl" of her youth (142): Bride has shrunk in size so that her clothes hang on her, and her underarm hair disappears, as does her pubic hair, her breasts, her pierced ears, and her periods.[1] To regain her former equilibrium, Bride realizes she must "discover what she was made of—cotton or steel—there could be no retreat, no turning back" (143). On her journey, the stable, loving white couple, Steve and Evelyn, along with the wounded, stray child they care for, Rain, enable Bride to develop empathy for other people during her forced convalescence in their remote and rustic cabin. Evelyn and Steve teach her to care for others with no strings attached or self-gain. They offer her care that is "free, without judgement" and offer love, laughter, and "pleasant memories shining in the looks they exchanged" (91). Overhearing Rain and Evelyn sing together, Bride thinks how nice it would have been to sing with her mother, rather than be shut off from her by a closed bathroom door. The singing of Evelyn and Rain uncovers this buried memory of loneliness and helps Bride to develop compassion for others.

While stranded at the cabin, Bride's interactions with Rain give her a better perspective on her own situation. Rain confides to Bride and feels protected by her, because "my black lady listens to me tell how it was. Steve won't let me talk about it. Neither will Evelyn" (104). Rain can heal only through testifying about her abuse to an empathetic listener, which she finds in Bride. When Rain describes her life on the streets, where anybody "could turn you in or hurt you" (103), her open vulnerability causes Bride to fight "against the danger of tears for anyone other than herself" (103). Her own vulnerability opens a feeling for Rain she has missed. Bride will put herself in harm's way to protect Rain from boys who taunt and threaten her, causing Rain to marvel, "nobody put their own self in danger to save me. Save my life. But that's what my black lady did without even thinking about it" (105–6). Bride has begun to feel emotions for others: first, guilt about Sofia Huxley; next, admiration at the warm happiness of Steve and Evelyn; then, compassion for Rain. Bride now relinquishes her own safe space to reach out to others. She does not think about her personal danger, not with her meeting with Sofia, not with her initial meeting of Booker and other pick-ups, not with driving her Jaguar into unknown places, and not with the basic-survival life of Steve and Evelyn and Rain. As she reaches outside of her own space, Bride becomes the outside listener who can help others heal. She grows from these interactions to heal herself in turn.

Booker's aunt, Queen, guides Bride in her quest to confront Booker and get to the meaning of his rejection. Queen provides the outside voice for Bride to build an inner one when she admonishes: "You come all this way and just turn around and leave?" Gaining strength, Bride proclaims, "You're absolutely right! Totally right! This is about me, not him. Me!" (152). Queen allows Bride to look inside herself and to fight for what she wants and needs. Bride realizes that "she had been scorned and rejected by everybody all her life. Booker was the one person she was able to confront—which was the same as confronting herself, standing up for herself. Wasn't she worth something? Anything?" (98). Confronting Lacan's "Real," Bride gathers her disparate pieces.

She physically attacks Booker so that he cannot escape a confrontation. They slap each other, and Bride breaks a bottle over his head—both using physical touch to initiate connection. Collapsed, Bride can confess to Booker that she lied under oath and wrongly convicted her teacher just so "my mother would hold my hand [...] And look at me with proud eyes, for once" (153). This truth provides Booker with the insight into Bride's actions he has lacked and enables him to verbalize his own trauma around his brother's death that caused him to desert her: "my brother was murdered by a freak, a predator like the one I thought you were forgiving" (154). Bride finishes the argument by stating, "It wasn't me who killed your brother [...] I was trying to make up to someone I ruined. You just ran around blaming everybody. [...] You don't have to love me but you damn well have to respect me" (154). Bride earns this respect by further sharing her guilt at not reporting the landlord's abuse of a young boy. Fearing eviction, Sweetness had commanded, "Don't say a word about it. Not to anybody" (54). When she tells Booker about this haunting secret, he comforts Bride by telling her that "you're not responsible for other folks' evil," helping to relieve the burden of remorse Bride has been carrying (55). Her testimony retrieves memories that allow Bride to see that "certain things I had buried came up fresh as though I was seeing them for the first time—how Sweetness's bedroom always seemed unlit"; uncovering repressed memory through testimony helps Bride mend (53).

By holding on to their childhood traumas, neither Bride nor Booker has fully lived in the present. Bride realizes that she never knew Booker or asked about *his* story; she focused solely on her own. It is only when Bride and Booker enter into a dialogue where they listen to each other's pain and commit to working together to heal each other that they can move forward. Bride will come to terms with her traumatic past in order to build self-love, and she will learn to love

Booker for the wounded person he is rather than an idealized partner who can rob her of her subjectivity when he shuts her out. Rather than the voice of her mother that makes Bride feel shame for her blackness, Booker tells Bride that her color is simply a "genetic trait—not a flaw, not a curse, not a blessing nor a sin" (143). Their exchange releases repressed memories they must confront. Once united with Booker on honest and open footing, Bride's adult body returns to help her move forward.

Booker has also come to terms with how he has hidden his grief, hoarding his pain to preserve his brother's presence in his life. By playing jazz music on his trumpet as a means of alleviating the trauma of his brother's abuse and murder, Booker had connected to a larger black community. He had insisted on keeping his brother's death an open wound not to be buried or forgotten. Although his family members had been close before the tragedy, sharing problems and a week's worth of learning every Saturday, their seeming willingness to move on isolates Booker, as there is no longer a forum to articulate grief as a group. When Booker listens to Bride's testimony about her painful childhood, he thinks "about how childhood cuts festered and never scabbed over" (134). In her presence, Booker can finally share the sorrow he has carried alone.

Having set their exchange in motion, Queen returns to see how the wounded lovers are doing, and she asks Booker what caused their split: "Lies. Silence. Just not saying what was true or why [...] About us as kids, things that happened, why we did things, thought things, took actions that were really about what went on when we were just children" (155). Queen not only listens to Booker but insists on asking hard questions in the safe space of her love for him. "She told her truth. What's yours? [Your brother] must be worn out having to die and get no rest because he has to run somebody else's life . [...] You managing him. [...] Did you ever feel free of him?" (157). As Queen leaves him to sort things out with Bride, she worries, "They will blow it [...] Each will cling to a sad little story of hurt and sorrow—some long-ago trouble and pain life dumped on their pure and innocent selves. And each one will rewrite that story forever, knowing the plot, guessing the theme, inventing its meaning and dismissing its origin" (159). But both Booker and Bride *do* process what Queen has unearthed, and they can get out of the endless cycle of mindlessly reliving childhood trauma. Robert Jay Lifton describes Booker's situation when he explains that for a survivor and witness,

> the only way one can feel right or justified in reconstituting oneself and going on living with some vitality is to carry through one's responsibility to the dead. And it's carrying through that responsibility via one's witness [...] that enables one to be an integrated human being once more. (12)

Booker carries on this responsibility by writing a note to his dead brother to articulate his pain at Adam's passing and his guilt at his own survival: "I miss the emotion that your dying produced a feeling so strong it defined me while it erased you leaving [...] I apologize for enslaving you in order to chain myself to the illusion of control" (161). His testimony to Adam helps him analyze his mourning behavior in order to live alongside his grief in the present.

Bride, in turn, "[h]aving confessed Lula Ann's sins [...] felt newly born. No longer forced to relive, no, outlive the disdain of her mother and the abandonment of her father" (162). Now, Bride and Booker "worked together like a true couple, thinking not of themselves, but of helping somebody else" (167). Booker discards his trumpet—the instrument he had taken up to express his sorrow—in a step toward starting over, feeling that music had served as the "displacement of loss" (174). He no longer needs the instrument to express his grief now that he has used words to do so. Caruth notes that the right listener helps the survivor in "producing a story [...] so that the internal addressee can come to create and to hear it as well" (49). Through his articulation with Bride, Booker has created an inner witness to validate the horror of Adam's death. When Bride tells Booker she is "pregnant and it's yours," Booker replies, "It's ours," solidifying his commitment to work on a future together (174).[2] Further, he "offered her the hand she had craved all her life, the hand that did not need a lie to deserve it, the hand of trust and caring for—a combination that some call natural love" (175). Bride and Booker can begin to envision a future.

But Morrison does not leave us with this sentimental ending. She closes the novel with the voice of Sweetness still rationalizing her treatment of her blue-black daughter and articulating the trauma she herself suffered under the gaze of white culture at Lula Ann's birth: "I know I did the best for her under the circumstances. When my husband ran out on us, Lula Ann was a burden. A heavy one but I bore it well" (177). Sweetness challenges Bride and Booker to do better as they are about "find out what it takes, how the world is, how it works and how it changes when you are a parent. Good luck and God help the child" (178). While readers listen to Sweetness's skepticism about the world she has known, they also witness the break-through of Bride and Booker and the possibility for their future progeny. Readers enter into "a dialogue with them, [so that] hearing about the experience from the mouths of those who have been victimized [produces] a deeper truth" (Lifton 19). Morrison's characters reveal stories "that cannot be told by someone else," and "the role of literature is to narrate this uncontainable" trauma (Felman 322, 334). Morrison draws in readers to witness the traumas of her characters in a sympathetic way, much like "the therapist expresses compassion and righteous indignation on behalf of the abused person" (Herman 143).[3] Having verbalized their traumas and pieced together their shattered selves, Bride and Booker have given testimony to what was unknown on a conscious level. Together, Bride and Booker, assisted by their community, have reconstructed their traumas to gain agency and self-esteem. For both of them, testimony that leads to the development of an inner listener provides necessary healing. They both move from objects to subjects, reclaiming selves that were shattered, reaching subject status through the dialogue of their inner and outer voices.

Notes

1. Laub's research shows that when "testimonies [were] not transmitted into a holding space, they remained fragmented and eventually were transformed into nightmares and into symptoms" (51). Bride's bodily transformations might be considered as symptoms that disappear when she and Booker create a holding space for their traumas.

2. According to Hartman, "telling [...] restores to the survivor who tells it this capacity to imagine a future" (231).

3. Cathy Caruth finds that what "returns to haunt the victim [...] is not only the reality of the violent event but also the reality of the way that its violence has not yet been fully known" (*Unclaimed* 5). Geoffrey Hartman claims that trauma is "an experience that is not experienced, that resists or escapes consciousness" (Hartman 214). In addition, talking "makes a connection, and it overcomes a terrible godforsaken loneliness that's part of the trauma story" (Van der Kolk 163). Art Blank writes that "part of what's traumatic about traumatic events is something about aloneness—being cut off, being alone" ("Apocalypse" 287).

Works Cited

Akinyela, Makunga M. "Narrative Therapy and Cultural Democracy: A Testimony View." *Australian and New Zealand Journal of Family Therapy*, vol. 35, 2014, pp. 46–49.

Atkinson, Yvonne. "Language That Bears Witness: The Black English Oral Tradition in the Works of Toni Morrison." *The Aesthetics of Toni Morrison: Speaking the Unspeakable*, edited by Marc C. Conner. UP of Mississippi, 2000, pp. 12–30.

Berg, Allison. "Trauma and Testimony in Black Women's Civil Rights Memoirs: *The Montgomery Bus Boycott and the Women Who Started It*, *Warriors Don't Cry*, and *From the Mississippi Delta*." *Journal of Women's History*, vol. 21, no. 3, 2009, pp. 84–107.

Blank, Arthur S., Jr., MD. "Apocalypse Terminable and Interminable: An Interview with Arthur S. Blank, Jr. Caruth, *Listening*, pp. 271–95.

———. "The One 'Who Testifies to an Absence': A Brief Review of the Psychoanalytic Study of the Effects of Extreme Trauma." Presentation at Scientific Meeting, Washington Psychoanalytic Society, Washington, DC. November 16, 2001.

Boles, Richard. "Documents Relating to African American Experiences of Congregational Churches in Massachusetts, 1773–1832. *New England Quarterly*, vol. 86, no. 2, 2013, pp. 310–23.

Caruth, Kathy, editor. *Listening to Trauma: Conversations with Leaders in the Theory and Treatment of Catastrophic Experience*. Johns Hopkins UP, 2014.

———. *Unclaimed Experience: Trauma, Narrative, and History*. Johns Hopkins UP, 1996.

Dorsey, Jennifer Hull. "A Documentary History of African-American Freedom: An Introduction to the Race, Slavery and Free Blacks Microfilm Collection." *Slavery and Abolition*, vol. 30, no. 4, 2009, pp. 545–63.

Felman, Shoshana. "A Ghost in the House of Justice: A Conversation with Shoshana Felman." Caruth, *Listening*, pp. 321–53.

Hartman, Geoffrey. "Words and Wounds: An Interview with Geoffrey Hartman." Caruth, *Listening*, pp. 213–35.

Herman, Judith, MD. "The Politics of Trauma: A Conversation with Judith Herman." Caruth, *Listening*, pp. 131–51.
hooks, bell. *Killing Rage*. Holt, 1995.
Hubert, Susan J. "Testimony and Prophecy in *The Life and Religious Experience of Jarena Lee*." *Journal of Religious Thought*, vol. 54/55, no. 2/1, 1998, pp. 45–52.
Lacan, Jacques. *Ecrits: A Selection*. Translated by Alan Sheridan. Norton, 1977.
———. *Four Fundamental Concepts of Psycho-Analysis*, edited by Jacques-Alain Miller. Translated by Alan Sheridan. Norton, 1981.
———. *The Seminar of Jacques Lacan: Book II, The Ego in Freud's Theory and in the Technique of Psychoanalysis 1954–1955*, edited by Jacques-Alain Miller. Translated by Sylvana Tomaselli. Norton, 1991.
Laub, Dori. "A Record That Has Yet to Be Made: An Interview with Dori Laub." Caruth, *Listening*, pp. 47–78.
Lifton, Robert Jay. "Giving Death Its Due: An Interview with Robert Jay Lifton." Caruth, *Listening*, pp. 3–22.
McGuire, Danielle. "'It Was Like All of Us Had Been Raped': Sexual Violence, Community Mobilization, and the African American Freedom Struggle." *Journal of American History*, vol. 91, no. 3, 2004, pp. 906–31.
Morrison, Toni. *God Help the Child*. Vintage International, 2016.
Murray, J-Glenn, SJ. "Let Talents and Tongues Employ: The Gift of Black African American Preaching." *New Theology Review*, vol. 23, no. 1, 2010, pp. 85–89.
Peretti, Burton W. "Speaking in the Groove: Oral History and Jazz." *Journal of American History*, vol. 88, no. 2, 2001, pp. 582–95.
Silverman, Kaja. *The Threshold of the Visible World*. Routledge, 1996.
Smitherman, Geneva. *Talkin That Talk: Language, Culture, and Education in African America*. Routledge, 2000.
Van der Hart, Onno. "The Haunted Self: An Interview with Onno van der Hart." Caruth, *Listening*, pp. 180–211.
Van der Kolk, Bessel A. "The Body Keeps Score: An Interview with Bessel van der Kolk." Caruth, *Listening*, pp. 153–77.
Visvis, Vikki. "Alternatives to the 'Talking Cure': Black Music as Traumatic Testimony in Toni Morrison's *Song of Solomon*." *African American Review*, vol. 42, no. 2, 2008, pp. 255–68.
Williams, Kidada E. *They Left Great Marks on Me: African American Testimonies of Racial Violence from Emancipation to World War I*. New York UP, 2012.

Childhood Traumas, Journeys, and Healing in Toni Morrison's *God Help the Child*

Mar Gallego[1]

In Morrison's works, traumatized children are victimized by the dreadful impact of racist and sexist stereotypes and their subsequent patterns of exclusion and marginalization. In many cases these childhood traumas are so severe that those children are unable to cope with them and eventually resort to madness and/or violence. However, in other cases, they learn to survive those traumatic experiences despite all odds and articulate a new sense of identity on their path to physical and psychological healing. My contention is that this is precisely the case in Morrison's final novel *God Help the Child* (2015), in which the author explores the limitations imposed by early trauma in her characters' lives and the diverse strategies of resilience they develop in order to overcome those limitations, thus facilitating reembodiment and self-empowerment.

Drawing from gender and intersectional studies, I argue that Morrison's *God Help the Child* delineates the coming into being of alternative female and male identities that are intrinsically dynamic and highly performative. The female protagonist, Bride, undergoes a suggestive transformation in order to confront her childhood traumas and claim her own voice and self. To do so, she will need to enact a mysterious journey back to her childhood to make sense of her present and give birth to a brighter future, both figuratively and literally, as she is pregnant at the end of the novel. Readers also witness the journey effected by Booker, Bride's boyfriend, who abandons her at the outset of the text. His is also a journey back to his childhood and his roots, involving a literal journey in order to reencounter his older self and come to terms with his brother's death. So both characters undertake a crucial journey that eventually leads to redemption and wholeness.

My reading of Morrison's text is informed by two main ideas that preside over the narrative of *God Help the Child*: on the one hand, the way in which the conflation of race and gender prejudice, together with sexual abuse and pedophilia, radically conditions and alters these characters' perceptions about themselves and their relationships to other characters in the novel. On the other hand, the importance of age in connection to the continuum between past and present is clearly revealed in the novel. Especially relevant is the way in which Morrison purposely blurs the distinction between past and present, childhood and adulthood, etc., in order to make readers reflect upon the contingent nature of human beings and the fluidity of identity markers, both at an individual and a collective level.

Black Femininities and Masculinities Reconstituted

In the novel the traditional codes of femininity and masculinity are questioned and subverted. Morrison insistently denounces the way in which these parameters are still focused on white manhood as the norm. To deconstruct this dominant model, it is necessary to take into account the multiple hierarchical systems of identification such as race, gender, class, sexuality, age, etc., that are crucial in redefinimg and reconceptualizing black femininities and masculinities within the framework of gender studies. As work by black feminist critics has repeatedly shown, the hegemonic model supported by white patriarchy is profoundly racist and sexist.[2] Morrison's novel revolves around this notion of white normativity, since most of the characters seem to subscribe to downright racist attitudes or to internalized racism, and to a gender-hierarchical system, whereby the male principle is still assigned all gender privileges. Indeed, the contemporary ideology of the new racism is built upon the replication of what intersectional analyses define as "intersecting oppressions" (Collins, *Black Sexual Politics* 121). Morrison's text examines these intersecting systems of oppression and the possibility of reformulating and contesting white hegemonic dominance.

Patricia Hill Collins insists on the use of an intersectional framework to understand "how racism and sexism were co-constituted, how class and heterosexism mutually constructed one another, and how citizenship status (nationality) is articulated with issues of ability and age" ("Foreword" viii). Moreover, as Lutz et al. assert, intersectionality has also provided "an instrument that helps us to grasp the complex interplay between disadvantage and privilege" (8). Intersectionality has then become an essential critical tool to comprehend the growing inequalities based upon race, class, gender, age, etc., which Morrison addresses in this work, especially, I would argue, the racialization and sexualization processes that ground stereotypical representations of the "other" and othered bodies. This system "draws much of its strength from the acquiescence of its victims, who have accepted the dominant image of themselves and are paralyzed by a sense of helplessness" (Pauli Murray cited in Collins, *Black Feminist Thought*, 99). Collins further claims that these additive systems of oppression are deeply rooted in the dichotomous Eurocentric and sexist ideology within the model of the matrix of domination, so "depending on the context, an individual may be an oppressor, a member of an oppressed group, or simultaneously oppressor and oppressed" (263). The way in which these systems of oppression are interconnected, especially how race and gender systems interact, is clearly reflected in the novel. In addition, I would further contend that Morrison uses intersectionality productively to underline the changing positions that juxtapose possibilities of being oppressed and oppressor at the same time.

To exemplify this latter statement is quite easy in the novel by means of a meditation upon how most characters can be described as occupying both positions at once. Especially clear is the case of Bride's mother, Sweetness, who is often both oppressor and oppressed, and sadly enough inflicts her own pain on her daughter. Adhering to a blind belief in internalized racism, Sweetness not only refuses to acknowledge her baby Lula Ann because of her dark skin but tries to suppress her in every conceivable way. She feels actual distaste and embarrassment as soon as she sets eyes on her. And these awful feelings lead her to thinking about actually giving her away or even attempting to suffocate the poor child: "I held a blanket over her face and pressed" (5). Lula Ann suffers not only from her mother's rejection but from her father's treatment as well; he regards her as an "enemy" from her birth, "never touched her" (5), and ends up leaving the baby without any regret, never looking back or trying to get in contact with her. The only sign of remorse is a fifty-dollar money order he regularly sends, basically to appease his conscience. The fact that both parents exhibit obvious symptoms of intracaste prejudice and parental disawoval makes the little baby's situation almost unlivable. For years throughout her childhood and youth, Lula Ann is forced to carry the burden of her father's abandonment and her mother's strict and loveless attitude. Indeed, never once do they acknowledge their faulty behavior toward their only daughter or make any attempt at apology.

But the notion that oppressed people become oppressors in turn can be also applied to other characters in the novel, who also fall prey to intracaste prejudice and act against the defenseless girl:

> Friends and strangers would lean down and peek in to say something nice and then give a start or jump back before frowning. That hurt. I could have been the babysitter if our skin colors were reversed. (6)

This scene clearly substantiates my interpretation by highlighting how Lula Ann's parents and many others at that time subscribed to the notion that light skin was superior, even endowing it with "dignity" (4) and social prestige, whereas dark skin is consistently identified with "a cross she will always carry" (7). The fact that intracaste prejudice is so deeply embedded within the fabric of black communities is an indication of how easily oppressed groups may turn into oppressors. As Fernanda Moore says, "racism, specifically that of light-skinned blacks toward dark-skinned," is one of several "Morrisonian themes" (60). This subservience to racist patriarchy is ultimately manipulated by the hegemonic status quo as a powerful instrument of oppression and rejection of its darker members. Colorism is therefore exposed as a crippling and distressing reality for people like Bride, who has to endure it for most of her childhood and youth.

Dark skin, with its negative connotations, is, however, not a static trope as a recurrent motif as the novel progresses. Indeed, what sets *God Help the Child* apart from other Morrison's novels like *The Bluest Eye* is precisely the double-sided take on color and race as it moves forward. Other black characters, in fact, do not play the role of oppressors over their oppressed group, and they convincingly object to colorism. For example, Booker states that black "is just a color ... a genetic trait—not a flaw, not a curse, not a blessing nor a sin" (143). He even invokes the scientific arguments that have undeniably proved the nonexistence of race,[3] thus disclosing how racism is "a choice" imposed by the powers that be as a justification for their discriminatory practices, and for their subsequent maintenance of social and political control. Conversely, Booker represents that other segment of African Americans, who do not advocate for intracaste prejudice and openly voice their condemnation of it. In line with this, he is fascinated by Bride's dark color, to the point that it could be argued that he is perhaps a bit too obsessed, too caught up with his ardent praise of dark color. As Hermione Hoby notes, "the novel intimates that fetishising blackness, both for the observer and the observed, might be as insidious as outright prejudice" (1). Nonetheless, his attitude highlights black communities' internal division regarding color and colorism, which Morrison is so intent on denouncing in her works.[4]

Besides, I would contend that Bride's dark skin is used by Morrison to postulate an understanding of race that persuasively resignifies the very notions of race and racism, allegedly inspired by the '60s motto "black is beautiful."[5] The way in which the character intentionally turns her darkness into her greatest asset is proof of a self-validating strategy that suggests other, more positive and healthier ways of inhabiting dark skin and blackness, both in the hegemonic society and in the African American community. This is especially revealing when the text registers how her "elegant blackness" raises "envy" or, even better, "glory" (57) not only among racist white people but also among those who have displayed notions of intracaste prejudice toward her in the past, as evidenced in the many hideous incidents throughout her childhood and youth narrated by Bride. In sum, the fact that Bride manages at times to force her blackness onto those who have stigmatized and tortured her in the past can be interpreted as a kind of revenge, or perhaps poetic justice in the novel. But it also calls attention to the need to end these discriminatory practices on the part of the dominant society but also among African Americans, whose system of values needs to be reevaluated and refashioned.

As I mentioned earlier on, in order to fully appreciate how to address the way in which the matrix of domination asserts its power in *God Help the Child*, attention needs to be directed not only to the insidious workings of racism but also to how sexism is instrumentalized by a certain number of the oppressed women in the novel. One interesting example is evidenced by Brooklyn, allegedly Bride's friend, when she reveals her opinions and choices in key scenes in the novel. The first one is related to Bride's cruel beating by the teacher Sofia. When Brooklyn comes to rescue Bride, she is presented as the ideal friend who is genuinely worried about Bride's well-being. Due to the brutality of the attack, Brooklyn readily believes that a man has tried to rape Bride. Even though she may harbor doubts about it, Brooklyn fulfills the role of the helpful best friend, comforting Bride on the way home. But her thoughts quickly betray her, as Brooklyn focuses on the advantages that her friend's helpless situation may entail for herself: "I shouldn't be thinking this. But her position at Sylvia, Inc. might be up for grabs" (26). Brooklyn adopts an attitude of competitiveness that signals an unmistakable adoption of an aggressive capitalist outlook on her part: she reproduces dominant parameters that allow her to make profit out of the terrible conditions of a friend, instead of focusing on the need for female bonding in response to trauma. The fact that Brooklyn is willing to discard her relationship with Bride shows a kind of shallow, callous woman who will jump at any opportunity for selfish reasons, without taking into consideration her friend's or other people's needs. She is a good representative of the successful corporate executive.

Her attitude is even more troubling when she attempts to seduce Booker, her friend's boyfriend, and in their own bed. She comes to their apartment unexpectedly, and upon finding him naked in bed, does not hesitate to jump right in without pausing to even ask.

Conventional patriarchal roles are exchanged when Booker refuses her, not violently but out of contempt for her. Their tense dialogue is a good testimony of this, as Bride asks:

> "Don't you want another flower in your garden?"
> ... "Are you sure you know what makes a garden grow?"
> "Sure I do ... Tenderness."
> "And dung." (59–60).

Her despicable behavior is called out by Booker, as another illustration of poetic justice. But it is my view that this exchange implies another reproduction of dominant parameters on her part. The fact that the hierarchical positions involved are not the traditional ones makes readers reflect upon the ways in which certain women also attempt to take advantage of the gender status quo, even appropriating sexist attitudes. Once again this is also a telling comment on how Brooklyn does not adhere to notions of female bonding and friendship, but rather to the idea of female rivalry for a desirable man, fostered by patriarchal stereotypical images of women. What is also striking in this scene is that Booker's desirability is described only in terms of his sexual appeal, as Brooklyn does not hold him in high esteem in any other regard. He does not seem to have material assets other than his body, which can also be read as another reversal of the sexual roles conventionally played by men and women. So Brooklyn also subjects Booker's body to a process of sexualization, usually assigned to women's bodies, materializing how the workings of sexism and racism are interdependent. In racial terms, Brooklyn seems to be pointing at the troubling history of the tense relationships between white women and black men; in this case a black man is the explicit object of desire on the part of a white woman.

Arguably, Brooklyn stands for a kind of woman who is keenly aware of the impact of the processes of racialization and sexualization to which black people are systematically subjected. Although she seems not to endorse this racist and sexist view, her actions betray a certain tendency to take advantage of the benefits, both material and sexual, that she can obtain from any situation propitiated by

Bride's absence. Her unethical behavior prevents the actual friendship and female bonding between them, exemplifying the divisive tactics capitalist patriarchal supremacy uses to control and contain women's ambitions and desires. Other similar cases from Morrison's novels come to mind, such as the warring Cosey women, Heed and Christine, in *Love*.

Sexual Abuse and Pedophilia Articulated

In addition to the denunciation of racism and sexism coherently argued by Morrison throughout *God Help the Child*, sexual abuse and pedophilia also provide another significant lens through which to resituate the system of interlocking oppressions that pervades the text, another indictment on Morrison's part to contest and reject their awful practices, in both the hegemonic and black scenarios. In fact, the novel is full of episodes of sexual assault on small children, and this is by no means an innocent choice by Morrison. In another chapter of this publication, critic Alice Knox Eaton delves into the connections between Morrison's first novel, *The Bluest Eye*, and this one. Among the clearest links between the two books are the instances of pedophilic mistreatment. However, what is utterly different here is the pervasiveness of illustrations that are narrated by diverse characters. The most paradigmatic cases in point are those of Bride and Booker, but Morrison also includes stories of pedophilia involving Brooklyn and the little girl Rain. The abundance of pedophilic episodes serves to highlight how contemporary society, far from protecting its young people, especially but not exclusively black girls and boys, exposes them to damage and corruption from a very early age. The recurrence of stories of sexual abuse of children censures an enduring white racist patriarchy that purposely condemns black (and other) children to degradation and sexual exploitation.

Bride is sadly aware of this kind of horrific behavior from a young age. Even before being instrumental in incarcerating the teacher Sofia for allegedly having abused children at her school, the novel reveals how the child Lula Ann witnesses her white landlord assaulting a child:

He was leaning over the short, fat legs of a child between his hairy white thighs. The boy's hands were fists, opening and closing. His crying was soft, squeaky and loaded with pain. . . . It was Mr. Leigh. He was zipping his pants while the boy lay whimpering between his boots. (54–55)

Mr. Leigh's sadistic cruelty and the boy's vulnerability are emphasized in the description, where the unnamed boy is easily identified with a pet or a baby, but undoubtedly too young to be subjected to this ignominy. The pedophile does not care about the pain and trauma he is inflicting on the child and exhibits no remorse when Lula Ann catches him. He calls her a "little nigger cunt!" (55), dismissing her further and demonstrating his complete lack of empathy or ethical principles. Moreover, what is even more disturbing is her mother's reaction when Lula Ann tells her. Instead of incriminating the pedophile, Lula Ann is forced by her mother to remain silent, resulting in this traumatic story haunting her over the years. As she puts it, "[Sweetness] wasn't interested in tiny fists or big hairy thighs; she was interested in keeping our apartment" (54). So Lula Ann is reprimanded a second time by an adult, in this case her mother, who does not defend the unguarded child that was molested, but rather becomes complicit with a system that allows such atrocities to happen. Being admonished by her mother, she will remain silent, and thus also an accomplice, until she finally tells her boyfriend Booker in a cathartic moment of the text. Sweetness's and Lula Ann's silences obviously speak volumes about the perpetuation of this terrible reality.

However, the text intimates that Bride finally testifies against Sofia as a result of both this previous trauma and her mother's dismissive attitude. At the end of the novel, the real intention behind her incomprehensible actions comes out in a crucial scene in which Booker questions her about buying presents for a child molester: "I lied! I lied! She was innocent. I helped convict her but she didn't do any of that" (153). While Bride's actions were guided by her need to make amends with the teacher, Sofia responds with violence. Consequently, Bride's confession throws light on the episode at several levels: first, her real motives of remorse are finally laid bare for having wronged a person's reputation and having ruined her life unconsciously, or so it seems. Justification for Bride's testimony can be obviously traced back to the conflicting relationship with her mother, because the girl never received the love she deserved or the affection she craved so desperately. This final confession unveils how the mother relentlessly mistreated her throughout her childhood, although Lula Ann made every effort to please her mother, even going to the extreme of blaming an innocent person of a horrendous crime to curry favor from her mother. Despite all her endeavors, she was consistently rejected by Sweetness. On another social plane, Bride's actions can be regarded as another rightful condemnation of the extremes to which racist patriarchy harms black children and their families, exacting a terrible toll on their harmonious living and their mutual understanding. These dysfunctionalities affect, in turn, society as a whole, and can lead to appalling cases such as Sofia's unjust punishment.

Focusing now on Booker's experiences with sexual abuse and pedophilia, it becomes obvious that he also has to overcome the trauma caused by his brother Adam's death. In that fateful conversation with Bride, he is finally able to face his terrible loss and articulate his painful existence afterward: "My brother, he was murdered by a freak, a predator like the one I thought you were forgiving" (154). Irony reverberates when this monster is described as "the nicest man in the world" (118), who tortured and maimed Booker's brother and many other unfortunate boys, even amputating their penises. Interestingly enough, readers are given minute details of the pedophile's actions, but his race is never revealed. The grisly details of the murders of Booker's brother and other victims circulated at the time of his trial, and the public exposure deeply disturbed Booker. The ghastly experience almost ruined Booker's relationship with the rest of the family. Booker tried to force his family to erect a memorial for the brother, but they refused, and as a result he was further estranged from them. Out of frustration and pain, he was unable to go on with his life, becoming the prototypical example of a "leaver" (146), as his beloved aunt Queen calls him. This also means that he is not at peace with himself, nor has he overcome his mourning. He will actually need Bride's confession to overcome the trauma of his brother's gruesome death.

Booker's subsequent violent reaction to child molesters is quite understandable. In college he beats a pedophile who was exposing himself near a park replete with children: "Booker's fist was in the man's mouth before thinking about it" (109). Later, he also attacks a couple who are smoking crack while their two-year-old child is crying and screaming in the car alone. In this case there are legal consequences, as the three of them are eventually arrested and Booker is given a "disturbing-the-peace ticket" by the judge (129). When his then-girlfriend, Felicity, asks him about the motivation behind this action, all he can say is that the baby was suffering, therefore becoming almost like a black "Catcher in the Rye," as it were.[6] Booker feels responsible for those vulnerable and unprotected children who can be attacked by "phony" adults and sadistic child molesters, and his mission is to save them, even from their own careless parents.

Having confessed their lies and secrets finally liberates both Bride and Booker and leads them to heal their festering wounds. Booker acknowledges that Bride's generosity to a supposed pedophile is what drove him away from her, so once again the connection between the past and the present is reactivated. At this moment it is evident how childhood traumas have strongly marked both their lives and their predicament since then, in having governed their behavior from childhood onward. As Bride's mother suggests in a moment of clarity: "What you do to children matters. And they might never forget" (43), clearly an indictment of what society allows to happen to children in general, but particularly to black children whose exposed lives are even more vulnerable and harsh.

Bad Mothers and Hurting Little Children

I would also argue that a complete account of traumatic childhood and the diverse systems of oppression at work in the narrative also needs to acknowledge the prominent role of mothers, especially as I have indicated above. As Aimable Twagilimana observes, "the African American (grand)mother is thus presented as a historian who keeps tradition in her songs and stories and teaches them to her children and grandchildren" (99). This role as cultural historian ensures the cultural heritage and survival of generations to come. However, Bride's mother, ironically called Sweetness, miserably fails to fulfill this mission and, by extension, can be defined as a "bad mother." Although she tries to justify her actions in the narration, her arguments are based on a clear strategy of internalized racism that does not allow her to actually love her child. As I have commented in the first section, from the very beginning of the novel she utters sentences such as "she was so black she scared me" (3). Being a high yellow woman, Sweetness deeply resents her dark-skinned daughter, whom she describes as a "throwback" (3) or a "burden" (177), reproducing demeaning racist stereotypes. In this sense, Sweetness clearly embodies toxic motherhood, exemplifying the ensuing effects of how "racism promotes a patriarchal authoritarian parenting style" (López-Ramírez 112). Her negative parenting style cannot provide the nurturance her child needs to thrive and severs any emotional bond between mother and daughter. Instead, her patriarchal motherhood is "about maternal control, compliance and conformity" (113), as Manuela López-Ramírez claims. She trains her daughter to fulfill the expectations of a racist society, without taking into account the damaging long-term impact on her daughter's psyche and body.

Many scholars have critiqued this African American authoritarian parental style resulting from the need to exercise control over the children so that they are obedient. hooks traces it back to "a model of parenting that mirrors the master-slave relationship" (*Sisters* 25). And she elaborates on this:

> These negative parental strategies were employed to prepare black children for entering a white-dominated society that our parents knew would not treat us well. They thought that by making us "tough," teaching us to endure pain with a stiff upper lip, they were ensuring our survival. (26)

Sweetness seems to align herself with this parenting model, as she affirms "the well-intended and, in fact, necessary way I brought her up" (177). But Sweetness's aloofness toward her daughter does not spring from her desire to protect her daughter, but from her own self-contempt and self-hatred. As Fatoumata Keita expresses it, she "deprives her only daughter of affection in order to preserve her privileged position, and thus abide by the dominant rule of class solidarity and racial purity" (45). Although by the end of the novel Sweetness knows that she is "the bad parent being punished," she still excuses herself by subscribing to patriarchal motherhood tainted by racist prejudice and its attending trauma.

The motif of the bad parent recurs in Morrison's novels, especially in *The Bluest Eye* with Pecola's mother but also in *Beloved*, where Sethe commits infanticide because she wants to save her children from bondage. In *God Help the Child*, other mothers fail to responsibly parent their children, either because they directly abuse or mistreat them, as in the cases of Rain or Queen's daughter Hannah,[7] or even murder them, like Julie, one of Sofia's inmates sentenced to prison for having killed her disabled daughter. After the crime Julie would spend her time in prison telling her dead daughter stories, ironically enough, mainly "fairy tales . . . all about princesses" (67). Her doing so truly reveals the distance between the world of fairy tales and little princesses, and little girls who can be murdered by their own mothers. Even in prison, "hurting little children" was seen as "the lowest of the low" (66), but in real life, stories accumulate about their extreme vulnerability and their complete lack of protection and shelter. It is not surprising after all this that Bride would feel "world-hurt" (83), representing all those traumatized children who have been rejected and badly mistreated in their childhood.

Bride, like Pecola, is "poisoned by rejection" (Furman and Wagner-Martin 18), by the lack of love and tenderness that she should have received from her mother. Not only that, Bride becomes the recipient of her mother's hatred and contempt for her own blackness that she despises and cannot come to terms with. Interestingly enough, when asked what prompted her to write this novel, Morrison also refers to the same notion of poison: "You're innocent. But you still have to deal with it. . . . I suspect there's always some little drop of poison" (Oatman 61). That poison annihilates Bride's self because of Sweetness's lack of understanding and empathy that eventually turns into Sweetness's major failure. Sweetness projects her own failure as a mother, and as a black woman, onto her child, using her as a scapegoat for all her fears about her own blackness.

So she is one more of those parents who victimize their children out of their "own despair and frustrations," out of their own "defeated lives" undone by racism and sexism (Furman and Wagner-Martin 15). However, the big difference between both characters is that Bride, unlike Pecola, is granted a voice and enough agency to recover from the pain and despair her mother is intent on transmitting to her, and is eventually able to effect a journey to self-affirmation and self-acceptance. Moreover, her mother's tainted love makes her react and search for real love, so all hope is not lost for these traumatized and mistreated children.

Redeeming the Past and Transforming the Future

In the end, the only way to redemption and healing for most characters in the novel is to go back to the beginning, that is, to go back to childhood literally as well as figuratively. It is not enough at this point to obsessively revisit the past as both Bride and Booker do constantly in the first phase of their relationship: whenever she tells him a painful memory, he comforts her, "knowing all about how childhood cuts festered and never scabbed over" (134). Both of them discover that childhood traumas do not disappear or hurt less if they are shared by some sympathetic person but continue to trouble them until they lose control over their lives and their actions. They need to confront those traumas but also each other, in order to actually find their true selves and be able to build a life together. Morrison often warns readers that the past cannot be forgotten, erased or conveniently buried; it has to be remembered and accounted for in order to effect an actual change at both the individual and collective levels. Arguably, Morrison's notion of "rememory" is crucial in this novel, as it activates strategies of resilience necessary to come to terms with the past.[8]

For Bride this rememory takes the form of a physical journey back to Lula Ann's little body, a sort of mystical trip that starts with significant alterations in her body: first she notices her earlobes are virgin once more (51), although she had them pierced when she was eight; she loses height and feels her body diminishing (81), her chest flattens (92), then her menstrual period gets delayed (95) until it stops completely, and her pubic hair also disappears (97), eventually making her understand "her crazed transformation back into a scared little black girl" (142). Her bodily transformation signals her need to confront those ghosts of the past in her present, especially that small girlish body that was repeatedly denied and negated. To acknowledge it, Bride is obliged to reinhabit it in order to get rid of the frustration and pain her neglected small body once endured.

Revisiting her child body enables Bride to find her true voice and real self. Henry Louis Gates identifies finding the true self as one of the themes of African American classics, and female classics in particular, speaking of "a young black woman finding her voice" (xxii), and this novel is the chronicle of the protagonist's evolution in the novel. Nevertheless, what is striking is that to find her voice, Bride needs to go back to her infancy and reshape what Gates calls "the ironies of individual and family history" (xxiii). So her memories help her to rewrite herself into being by coming to terms with those ironies and putting them to rest. The process involved is not only shocking for the character, it is also extremely symbolic as Bride's embodied regression into the past.

Apart from the bodily changes Bride experiences, she also embarks on a road trip that results in an accident, forcing her to stay with a white hippie family for six weeks. Reverting into a little girl, after the car accident, she is taken care of by a white family, especially the mother Evelyn and the daughter Rain, who can remind readers of Amy in *Beloved*: "milk-white skin, ebony hair, neon eyes, undetermined age" (86).[9] Bride feels utterly helpless and in need of assistance, finally turning into a needy child who is "adopted" by the white family whose welcome song is quite significant: "This land is your land, this land is my land . . ." (87).[10] Their home clearly becomes a refuge, "a coffin" (92), indicating the need for a rebirth. The fact that Bride has reached the bottom of her helplessness and her vulnerability is also pointed out by her lack of mobility, as if she had become a baby that needs to be carried around by the surrounding adults.

The sponging ritual that is enacted throughout the stay also marks a turning point in Bride's transformation, since she is bathed by a white woman who does not show any reluctance to touch her emaciated body, quite contrary to her own mother's constant dismissal. For Evelyn, Bride's blackness is not configured as a threat, just as a fact, just as a color like the rest of them, much in line with Booker's previous affirmations. It is interesting to see how the text does not portray all white people as racist in the novel, as Evelyn even welcomes intimacy with a black body that is dutifully respected and caressed. Besides, it could be contended, too, that Evelyn performs this sponging ritual as part of Bride's healing ritual back to life through the enjoyment provided by being touched by another human being. This human touch is allegedly another way of restoring Bride back to health and wholeness, since her body is configured once again as her private possession, under her control, instead of being understood as a public property to be used and abused by vicious mothers and sadistic pedophiles. The sanctity of her own body is thus reestablished in the narration as the main premise on which to formulate a new understanding of self-identity and self-worth.

Another important aspect of Bride's recovery is the companionship she feels with Rain, a companionship "surprisingly free of envy. Like the closeness of schoolgirls" (103). Rain arguably represents the best friend Bride grew up without, so her friendship is another step on the way to rewriting and correcting her childhood story of suffering and isolation. In many of Morrison's novels, two close friends are the main protagonists, and the way in which their relationship develops throughout the years is one of the main ideas presiding over the text.[11] Female bonding is undoubtedly crucial for a healthy development of women's psyches from early childhood, as it helps them to make sense of the changes they undergo and of the world around them. Indeed, Morrison hints at the importance of female bonding in each of her novels, but also at the danger of isolation as one of the greatest risks run by girls and women in a racist and sexist society. Again, Pecola can be conjured here as the extreme example of the unforeseen consequences of loneliness and grief for a little girl who feels utterly rejected by everybody in that black community, including her own dysfunctional parents. At the beginning of *God Help the Child*, Bride is presented as a successful businesswoman with an intense social life, with friends, especially with a really good friend, Brooklyn. As the novel unfolds, this facade starts to crumble to pieces, and Bride's bleak reality of confusion and solitude is gradually revealed. These feelings are exacerbated when her difficult relationship with her mother takes full form in the novel.

The journey to Bride's childhood can be construed as an essential corrective to her dreary young existence, as for the first time in her life she feels true companionship, in her relationship with Rain. This friendship transforms Bride and enables her to show empathy without being hurt or punished for it, probably also for the first time. The feeling is reciprocated by Rain, who has also had her own share of pain at the hands of another reprobate mother. Bride protects Rain from some violent boys who wanted to hurt her, and her sacrifice finally seals their union: Rain reflects, "[N]obody had done that before [...] put their own self in danger to save me. Save my life" (106). The fact that Bride would willingly risk her own security for her friend textualizes the close bond that ties them together. Besides, they also feel confident enough to verbalize all their nightmarish traumas and experiences to the other, which is another indication of the special connection to each other. Their encounter acquires great resonance in the novel, since it contributes to break the pattern of isolation and self-destruction both characters were burdened by before their encounter. Eventually their companionship launches these two stigmatized characters onto their path to physical and psychic recovery.

For Booker, it is different, as he always had a companion from childhood, his beloved brother Adam, before he became paralyzed by the trauma of his death. When he finds the strength to let go of that burden after his significant conversation with Bride, he is able to follow the passage to actual reconciliation with his memories, which makes him ready to plan a future with her. By the end of the novel, both characters have developed their resilient strategies and seem to understand the importance of coming to terms with the past, to be able to make sense of their present and to foresee a better future. The unborn child in Bride's womb symbolizes that new beginning, that new possibility of starting anew, to correct past mistakes and to finally live in peace. But the unborn child is also another chance for the society as a whole, and for black communities in particular, to undo their misdeeds, as it were. The baby fosters the vision of a more holistic way to deal with racial and gender issues, which can be construed as a hopeful alternative that manages to deconstruct, and eventually do away with, the interlocking systems of oppression that continue to marginalize, denigrate, and suffocate the lives of black children and, by extension, of the black community. The only way to heal those wounds, Morrison intimates, is to place black children at the heart of communal care and love.

Notes

1. The author wishes to acknowledge the funding provided by the Spanish Ministry of Science, Innovation and Universities (Research Project "Bodies in Transit 2," ref. FFI2017-84555-C2-1-P), the European Regional Development Fund, and the Spanish Research Agency for the writing of this essay.

2. Commenting on the representations of black people in the mass media, bell hooks states, "Those images may be constructed by white people who have not divested of racism, or by people of color/black people who may see the world through the lens of white supremacy—internalized racism" (*Black Looks* 1).

3. The UNESCO meetings took place in the '50s and '60s, issuing several declarations to publicly proclaim the lack of scientific validation to support claims for different races. See for instance, Ivan Hannaford's *Race: The History of an Idea in the West* (1996) for an interesting discussion of the debates that were generated.

4. Starting from her first novel, *The Bluest Eye*, this denunciation can be observed in varying degrees in most of Morrison's narratives.

5. Other critics like Hoby invoke *Tar Baby* as the novel's precedent, because of the focus on a contemporary setting, but Hoby also adds that *God Help the Child* is "a reflection of the increasing superficiality of our moment."

6. Recalling the protagonist's need to protect innocent children in J. D. Salinger's classic.

7. Rain confesses to Bride how she was thrown out of the house because she bit a man's penis when constrained to prostitution by her own mother (101); Queen's daughter Hannah, presumably abused by her own father, tells her mother about it, but the woman refuses to believe her (170).

8. Especially in Morrison's haunting *Beloved*, but this is one of Morrison's main themes in all her novels.

9. Although not described in detail, Amy is firstly identified as "a whitegirl" with "thin little arms but good hands ... hair enough for five heads" (77). Yet by

the end of the scene, she is depicted as "a barefoot whitewoman" (85), so her age remains uncertain.

10. The text of the song convincingly recalls both the American anthem and Langston Hughes's poem "I Too," especially bringing to the forefront fundamental issues of belongingness and identity.

11. *Sula* (1973) is one recurrent model in Morrison's oeuvre; indeed, I would contend that this novel is a precursor of later novels. Sula and her alter ego Nel's conflictive and symbiotic relationship is chronicled from infancy to their mature years. Another instance is *Love* (2003), where two intimate friends, Christine and Heed, are dramatically separated by Christine's grandfather's shocking decision to marry eleven-year-old Heed, a decision that will mark the two girls' lives well into maturity.

Works Cited

Collins, Patricia Hill. *Black Feminist Thought: Knowledge, Consciousness, and the Politics of Empowerment*. Unwin Hyman, 1990.

———. *Black Sexual Politics: African Americans, Gender, and the New Racism*. Routledge, 2005.

———. "Foreword: Emerging Intersections—Building Knowledge and Transforming Institutions." *Emerging Intersections: Race, Class and Gender in Theory, Policy and Practice*, edited by Bonnie T. Dill and Ruth E. Zambrana. Rutgers University Press, 2008, pp. vii–xiii.

Furman, Jan, and Linda Wagner-Martin. *Toni Morrison's Fiction: Revised and Expanded Edition*. U of South Carolina P, 2014.

Gates, Henry Louis. "What Is an African American Classic?" *12 Years a Slave*, by Solomon Northup. Penguin, 2013, pp. xv–xxiv.

Hannaford, Ivan. *Race: The History of an Idea in the West*. Woodrow Wilson Center Press, 1996.

Hoby, Hermione. "Toni Morrison: I'm Writing for Black People . . . I Don't Have to Apologize; As Her Latest Book *God Help the Child* Is Published, the Nobel Prizewinner Talks about the Danger of Beauty, Supporting Hillary and Earning the Right to Say Shut Up." *Guardian*, 1 May 2015. Accessed 12 September 2018.

hooks, bell. *Black Looks: Race and Representation*. South End Press, 1992.

———. *Sisters of the Yam: Black Women and Self-Recovery*. 1994. Routledge, 2015.

Keita, Fatoumata. "Conjuring Aesthetic Blackness: Abjection and Trauma in Toni Morrison's *God Help the Child*." *Africology*, vol. 11, no. 3, 2018, pp. 43–55.

López-Ramírez, Manuela. "'What You Do to Children Matters': Toxic Motherhood in Toni Morrison's *God Help the Child*." *Grove*, no. 22, 2015, pp. 107–19.

Lutz, Helma, Maria Teresa Herrera Vivar, and Linda Supik, editors. *Framing Intersectionality: Debates on a Multi-Faceted Concept in Gender Studies*. Ashgate e-books, 2011.

Moore, Fernanda. "*God Help the Child*: A Novel." *Culture & Civilization*, April 2015, pp. 69–70.

Morrison, Toni. *God Help the Child*. Alfred A. Knopf, 2015.
———. *Beloved*. Picador, 1987.
———. *The Bluest Eye*. Washington Square Press, 1970.
———. *Love*. Chatto & Windus, 2003.
———. *Tar Baby*. Signet, 1981.
———. *Sula*. Plume, 1973.
Oatman, Maddie. "The New Black: Nobel Winner Toni Morrison on Fashion, Ghosts and the Paper Bag Test." *Mother Jones*, vol. 40, no. 3, 2015, pp. 60–62.
Twagilimana, Aimable. *Race and Gender in the Making of African American Literary Tradition*. Garland, 1997.

"Let the True Note Ring Out Loud": A Mindful Reading of *God Help the Child*

Susana Vega-González

> *One person cannot awaken another. No God can awaken someone. No belief can awaken someone. No meditation can awaken someone. The individual's transformative understanding is their awakening... the realistic understanding that liberates is the individual's own process and attainment.*
>
> ROBERT THURMAN

In her 1996 acceptance speech for the National Book Foundation Medal for Distinguished Contribution to American Letters, "The Dancing Mind," Toni Morrison deals with the necessity of isolation and silence in the acts of reading and writing, a state in which the writer's mind and the reader's mind can embrace in a metaphorical dance. To illustrate this, she refers to a particular case of a PhD student who found great difficulty in just sitting in a room by himself to read for hours, with no distractions or companionship from anyone but himself. What Morrison is addressing here is exactly a cultural handicap of the modern Western world that has reached our current societies: the inability to cultivate and appreciate silence and inner landscapes. In a technological era dominated by social media and all sorts of devices supposedly created to improve human lives and communication, contemplative silent moments are hard to find and harder to foster, thus leading to an existence like the reader Morrison refers to, "disabled by an absence of solitude" ("Dancing" 190).

Although silence is commonly associated with the ideas of oppression and dispossession, it can also be a powerful tool conducive to self-knowledge, rebirth, and catharsis. When the dynamics of power are at work, silence can have both positive and negative implications, depending on whether such silence is imposed or chosen. Throughout both her fiction and her nonfiction, Toni Morrison has dealt with the implications of silence on numerous occasions. The very first novel she published, *The Bluest Eye*, begins with a direct reference to silence: "Quiet as it's kept." And in *God Help the Child* (2015), one of the characters states after being released from prison, "I don't think many people appreciate silence or realize that it is as close to music as you can get. Quiet makes some folks fidget or feel too lonely. After fifteen years of noise I was hungry for silence more than food" (69). In this light, Carolyn Denard's essay "Some to Hold, Some to Tell: Secrets and the Trope of Silence in *Love*" is illustrative of how the politics of silence has played an important role in the African American community. As Denard contends, "within the black community, keeping silent ... is also a form of protection emanating from an ethic of care" (91).

In her Remarks Given at the Howard University Charter Day Convocation (1995), Toni Morrison addresses the process through which the machinery of racism is created and implemented, based on some carefully designed pillars that grant, first of all, the existence of a constructed enemy (both exterior and interior) and then the manipulation of the enemy's image. One of those pillars, as Morrison explains is "mindlessness" (167). By rewarding mindlessness and apathy, the racist machinery is engrained in the society and in the enemy's mind. The alledged inferiority of the enemy will thus be engraved and institutionalized. The last of those pillars, Morrison argues, is silence: "Last, maintain at all costs silence" (167).

The present essay aims to shed new light on the critical analysis of silence and offer a new dimension of chosen silence as one of the diverse integral parts of the opposite of the mindlessness Morrison indicts in her remarks, that is, mindfulness. Silence is addressed here not as an undesirable crippling tool of oppression but as a source of power. The mindful reading of Morrison's novel this essay suggests will prove that healing and empowerment can be achieved as much through silence as through speech; it will also demonstrate how silence is a breeding ground for potentiality and a conveyor of meaning. The main focus of this analysis is placed on *God Help the Child*, as it reveals numerous direct and implicit manifestations of mindfulness.

Silence is the basis for inner knowledge and enlightenment. From silence comes personal introspection, a dance with the self, which is so necessary for personal growth and catharsis. This emphasis on silence together with the fact that for Morrison the culmination of a story resides in the moments when its characters understand something and acquire knowledge calls for a detailed analysis of this work from a mindful perspective. As Morrison contends, "A lot of books are about winning something. I'm not interested in that so much as the way the intellectual life and the emotional life should be" (Manyika 147). To a greater or lesser extent, Morrison's novels encapsulate the maxims of mindfulness: awareness of the present moment, compassion and kindness, love and self-love, gratitude, forgiveness, introspection, self-knowledge, understanding, and acceptance. All or most of these elements are usually at work in the multiple cases of trauma that abound in Morrison's works. But if we had to choose one single piece and passage that represents the essence of mindfulness, we would select Baby Suggs's memorable speech at The Clearing in *Beloved*, which can be read as the quintessential expression of mindfulness. If we peruse the passage carefully—mindfully—we can identify some of the key elements of mindfulness—here, now, awareness, acceptance, attention to the body, and self-love, once again, amidst a chosen silence:

> Baby Suggs bowed her head and prayed silently. [. . .] Let the children come! . . .
> "*Here*," she said, "in this *here* place, we flesh; [. . .] flesh that dances on bare feet in grass. Love it. Love it hard. [. . .] Love your hands! Love them. Raise them up and kiss them. [. . .] More than your life-holding womb and your life-giving private parts, *hear me now*, love your heart. For this is the prize." (87–89; my emphasis)

That Baby Suggs mentions all the body parts (hands, mouth, face, feet, liver, lungs, heart, etc.) is reminiscent of a mindfulness practice called "body scan," where the focus is placed on the body, paying attention to each one of its parts as a kind of anchor to the present moment. "Here" and "now" are probably the most significant words in mindfulness, as this practice revolves around conscious awareness of the here and the now.

As it happens, in several of Morrison's novels, characters undergo the effects of traumatic experiences. Pecola Breedlove, Shadrack, Sethe, Frank and Cee Money, and Booker Starbern are some instances. Their trauma triggers mechanisms of defense such as the blockage of feelings or memories or the weaving of self-protective lies. In some cases these characters demonstrate a clear lack of awareness, acknowledgment and acceptance of feelings and memories related to past traumas. However, after a metaphorical and physical journey, and usually with the assistance of an ancestor figure, those characters finally heal and recover. The journey proceeds from traumatic memory to narrative memory, just as, after a period of rest and silence, understanding, learning and acceptance take place. In this light, leading mindfulness scholar Jon Kabat-Zinn argues that "coming to terms with things as they are is my definition of healing" (Kabat-Zinn).

Both protagonists of *God Help the Child* struggle with past traumatic memories and, in the case of Bride, the additional heavy weight of a lie. Although narrating traumatic memories is essential to revision and healing, the silence that necessarily precedes such narrative is equally crucial. Bride finally deals with and speaks her childhood lie, after having hidden it for years. Healing and rebirth follow. Therefore, Bride moves from a state of mindlessness to a renewed state of mindfulness. And such a change takes place through the recurrent image of the journey and in an equally recurrent setting for the healing of traumatized characters: nature or a rural setting. It is worth noting here that mindfulness practice is deeply connected to and feeds upon elements in nature; and this is why mindfulness retreats are usually set in a natural or rural location. This movement from mindlessness to mindful awareness is accurately portrayed in one of the unpunctuated passages Booker writes to channel his thoughts while he is in a relationship with Bride:

> You accepted like a beast of burden the whip of a stranger's curse and the *mindless* menace it holds along with the scar it leaves as a definition you spend your life refuting although that hateful word is only a slim line drawn on a shore and quickly disolved in a seaworld any moment when an equally *mindless* wave fondles it like the accidental touch of a finger on a clarinet stop that the musician converts into *silence in order to let the true note ring out loud.* (149–50; my emphasis)

The idea behind this paragraph is obviously racism, the "whip of a stranger's curse." The passage also refers to the mindless acceptance of racism, as a given condition, unquestioned by the racist oppressor and internalized by the oppressed and victimized. These unquestioned ideas are ingrained in brains as deeply as the ongoing chatter that inhabits minds in a racist world, and they are due to a combination of mindless emotions and feelings, the most powerful of which is fear—fear of the different one, the Other. Fear that leads to rejection. Hence, fear and rejection of oneself.

Racism is the underlying evil that triggers some of the characters' feelings, emotions, and behavior. From racism stems "the harm of racial self-loathing" (Morrison, *Origin* 14) that conditions Sweetness, her husband, and, later on, Bride. The internalized racism to which Morrison had straightforwardly devoted her debut novel, *The Bluest Eye*, is revisited in *God Help the Child*. In her recent work *The Origin of Others*, Morrison once again explores the underpinnings of scientific racism as the identification of an outsider, an Other, which becomes necessary to define one's self (6), the ultimate goal being the exertion of dominance, power, and control over the Other. The politics of racism are based on skin color, and thus skin turns into "a definitive mark of acceptability" (64). Color coding and labeling determine the degree of acceptability and the options for potentially passing as white. Indeed, in the beginning of *God Help the Child*, a light-skinned black mother gives birth to a "blue-black" baby that she internally rejects from the moment she sees her skin color. The mother, ironically called Sweetness, apologetically exonerates herself from having birthed such a baby and experiences feelings of disdain and detachment from her daughter: "It's not my fault. So you can't blame me. [...] [S]omething was wrong. Really wrong. She was so black she scared me. [...] I'm light-skinned, with good hair. [...] Some of you probably think it's a bad thing to group ourselves according to skin color—the lighter, the better. [...] But how else can we hold on to a little dignity?" (3–4).

The opening of the novel revolves around the ideas of blame and the dichotomy wrong/bad versus right/good. Just because of the skin color, Sweetness is shamed and embarrassed by her baby. This in turn triggers an absence of proper motherly love and affection. The child, Lula Ann, grows so desperately lovelorn, so much in need of feeling her mother's and father's touch—her father never touched her either—that she resorts to a lie that finally results in her mother's holding her hand for the first time, when she is eight years old. By testifying against an innocent female teacher accused of child molestation, Lula Ann finally makes her mother proud instead of ashamed:

> I glanced at Sweetness; she was smiling like I've never seen her smile before. [...] As we walked down the courtroom steps she held my hand, my hand. She never did that before and it surprised me as much as it pleased me because I always knew she didn't like touching me. [...] I used to pray she would slap my face or spank me just to feel her touch. (31)

Abandoned by her father and emotionally forsaken by her mother, Lula Ann desperately desires love and connection. Her childhood trauma is increased by her remorse at having helped condemn an innocent person, Sofia Huxley. But Bride (Lula Ann) is not the only tormented character in the novel. Her boyfriend Booker is also prey to childhood trauma marked by the sexual murder of his beloved brother. Bride's friend Brooklyn also had to leave home when she was only fourteen years old; her alcoholic mother and the dubious intentions of an uncle made her run away and fend for herself. She claims, "I invented myself" (140). Another character, Rain, is raised by a prostitute mother who gets money from men who have sexual dealings with her child. But Rain is eventually thrown out by her mother. Homeless and without a family, she has to take care of herself and survive until she is found by a couple, Steve and Evelyn, who take her with them and become her only family. Even Queen, Booker's old aunt, is haunted by a feeling of blame for not believing her daughter when she reported having been molested by Queen's husband.

This novel is peopled by fragmented characters, too often at odds with themselves and fraught with memories of past events that lie hidden in their minds. These characters resort to a kind of emotional shield as a tool of self-protection and survival in the form of secrets and lies, either to themselves or to others. In the case of Sweetness, her unconscious feeling of blame for having been so hard on her daughter is assuaged by her lying to herself, telling herself that the intention behind her toughness was to protect her daughter: "I wasn't a bad mother, you have to know that, but I may have done some hurtful things to my only child because I had to protect her. Had to. All because of skin privileges" (43). Bride hides the truth about Sofia Huxley from others. Not even Booker knows that the alleged child molester was actually innocent and never should have been charged with the crime. As a result of that maintained lie, Booker abandons Bride when he sees she wants to give money and presents to the ex-convict. All these traumatic experiences translate into internal mental noise and undesired memories. As Bride herself realizes, "[m]emory is the worst thing about healing" (29).

These traumatic memories are often portrayed in a somatic manner, in close association with the body. A common metaphor used is that of the scar or scab: "childhood cuts festered and never scabbed over" (134) or "the scar it leaves" (149), referring to racism and its consequences as well as to childhood sexual assault. As is often the case in Morrison's fiction, characters appear emotionally scarred, to a greater or lesser extent. But since there is no dividing line between mind and body in the human being, those emotional scars are often transposed onto the body. Hence, Bride experiences an erasure of her bodily signs of female adulthood. Her pubic and armpit hair disappears, her chest becomes flat, her period disappears, too, and her earlobes return to their unpierced state. She patently regresses to the stage of childhood, which can be interpreted as Bride's dealing with her childhood trauma in her process of healing. This is a clear case of "somatic reenactments of the undigested trauma" that affects victims of trauma (Van der Kolk 101). And in order to heal, the past trauma must be revisited, understood, and reconfigured so that it does not interfere with the pursuit of present happiness. Therefore, healing starts with both the mind and the body.

As Bessel Van der Kolk contends in *The Body Keeps the Score*, "[s]elf-regulation depends on having a friendly relationship with your body. Without it you have to rely on external regulation—from medication, drugs like alcohol, constant reassurance, or compulsive compliance with the wishes of others" (97). Since racism deeply conditions and determines Bride's childhood and her mother's relationship with her, Bride is estranged from her body and her self, to the point of admitting she is not the person she would like to be. When Booker breaks up with her on the grounds that she is not the woman he wants, she automatically replies, "Neither am I" (8), realizing "I still don't know why I said that. It just popped out of my mouth" (8). Although Bride has learned to use her blackness to her own benefit in a world where blackness can be, and is, commodified, she nonetheless keeps unconscious track of the profound sense of deficiency her mother had instilled in her because of her skin color. Indeed, her ritual covering her face with the white foam left behind by her abandoning boyfriend is indicative of her unconscious wish for white skin or a lighter type of black. Whiteness is clearly associated with acceptance, rightness, and affection or love: "Slathering the foam on my face I am breathless. I lather my cheeks, under my nose. [...] I stare at my face. My eyes look wider and starry. My nose is not only healed, it's perfect, and my lips between the white foam look so downright kissable. [...] I don't want to stop" (35). Enjoying the whitened face on the mirror seems to be a source of relief for Bride, who goes even further when she admits, "[W]hen I feel depressed the cure is tucked away in a little kit where his shaving equipment is. Lathering warm soapy water, I can hardly wait for the brushing and then the razor, the combination that both excites and soothes me. Lets me imagine without grief times when I was made fun of and hurt" (35). It is precisely for these reasons that Bride's healing must start with focused attention to her body in the present moment. As Van der Kolk concludes, "[p]hysical self-awareness is the first step in releasing the tyranny of the past" (101). According to this psychiatrist and expert in post-traumatic disorders, it is imperative for victims of trauma to become aware of and befriend the sensations in their bodies by, first of all, noticing and describing their bodily feelings and then labeling them, which in scientific jargon is called "interoception," so "the greater our awareness, the greater our potential to control our lives. Knowing *what* we feel is the first step to knowing *why* we feel that way. [...] This is why mindfulness practice [...] is a cornerstone of recovery from trauma" (95).

Bride becomes aware of her regression in time through the changes in her body. Not only that, but she acknowledges those sensations associated with her body: "I'm scared. Something bad is happening to me. I feel like I'm melting away. I can't explain it to you but I do know when it started" (8); when she describes her "baby thumb earlobes" she says, "I'm trembling" (51); she continues to further describe her bodily sensations, being aware of the calmness she feels after she lathers her hairless armpits, all of which is followed by her consciousness of her thoughts: "Calmed, I go back to bed and slide under the sheet. Minutes later my head explodes with throbbing pain. I get up and find two Vicodins to swallow. Waiting for the pills to work there is nothing to do but let my thoughts trail, track and bite one another" (53).

Not only does Bride observe her body, her feelings, emotions, and sensations, but she also accepts—allows—the surge of thoughts that flood her mind. She further looks inside herself and inquires about her state by asking herself these questions: "What is happening to me?" and "What's going on? I'm young; I'm successful and pretty. [...] So why am I so miserable?" (53) or the question "Why am I still sad?" (34). She wants to know not only what the problem is but the reasons behind it. Those questions represent the internal investigation required for proper healing and are a cornerstone of mindfulness, together with awareness and acceptance. Mindful awareness of the body can also be exercised in conjunction with a wider awareness of the physical surroundings where the body is at a given moment. The park scene where Bride sits on a bench and observes a silent couple walking by is a passage of profound mindfulness, an implied message that does not go unnoticed by Bride:

> I select a bench near an artificial pond where real ducks sail. [...] I hear slow steps on gravel. I look up. The steps belong to a gray-haired couple strolling by silent, holding hands. [...] Both wear colorless slacks and loose T-shirts imprinted with faded signs [...] about peace. [...] The couple moves carefully, as though in a dream. Steps matching, looking straight ahead like people called to a spaceship where a door will slide open and a tongue of red carpet rolls out. They will ascend, hand in hand, into the arms of a benevolent Presence. (39)

The vocabulary and content of this passage describe the very essence of mindfulness: "slow," "silent," "bench," "carefully," "peace," "space"-ship are followed by the ultimate key word in mindfulness, "Presence."

Nature always plays an important role in the healing of Morrison's characters, and metaphors and symbols involving natural elements occur frequently. Bride's trip to a rural town in search for Booker will prove to be a true initiatory journey into healing and understanding similar to the one Milkman Dead takes in *Song of Solomon*. Driving her Jaguar on the way to Whiskey, she crashes against "what must have been the world's first and biggest tree" (82). The allusion to the Tree of Life, as a symbol of life and regeneration, comes to mind immediately and leads Bride into a true rite of passage. However, Bride cannot yet identify with or feel soothed by natural elements, as she is still at the beginning of her geographical and metaphorical journey. Thus, the tree limbs that Morrison has previously equated to motherly figures of protection and love in other novels frighten Bride:

> The moon was a toothless grin and even the stars, seen through the tree limb that had fallen like a throttling arm across the windshield, frightened her. The piece of sky she could glimpse was a dark carpet of gleaming knives pointed at her and aching to be released. She felt world-hurt—an awareness of malign forces changing her from a courageous adventurer into a fugitive. (83)

Bride's fear of and disconnection from nature is reminiscent of that of Jadine Childs in *Tar Baby* when she gets caught in a swamp and tries to fight the swamp women hanging from the trees. Likewise, Bride appears terrified by the silence that surrounds her, which is highly symptomatic: "the surrounding trees coming alive in the dawn really scared her, and the silence was terrifying" (84). These descriptions make it clear that Bride is a true fugitive on the run from herself, from her past, and from the primal connection to nature, of which she is a part. This lack of acknowledgment and absence of true knowledge evince the spiritual ailment Bride is affected by. At this stage, Bride "knows nothing (as yet) of kindness and compassion" (Walker), as her success in the world of fashion and cosmetics has placed her in the mindless wheel of consumerism and money.

In his seminal book *Silence*, Thich Nhat Hanh explains that silence is necessary to look deep inside ourselves to explore our feelings and emotions, as silence creates the necessary space and clarity for that purpose. Silence is the conduit to establishing lost connections with ourselves and with the natural world to which we belong. All the daily distractions and materialist pursuits that are so highly sought after in order to fill our lives are but covers that hide and avoid necessary encounters with ourselves: "Many of us are afraid of going home to ourselves because we don't know how to handle the suffering inside us. That's why we're always reaching for more and more sense impressions to consume" (Nhat Hanh, *Silence* 30). As a result of the Jaguar crash, Bride has a wonderful—albeit difficult—opportunity to start facing herself alone, in silence.

Rain, a racially ambiguous adolescent girl, finds Bride; soon after, a man comes to rescue Bride and take her to his house, which is also Rain's home. Even when she is rescued by Steve, silence dominates the scene: "Silently, asking no questions and offering no verbal comfort, he positioned her in his arms" (84–85). The power of silent comforting action supersedes the power of words. The period of six weeks Bride spends at their house proves to be a rite of passage not only into physical healing but also into understanding, knowledge, and renewal. In mindfulness terms it could even be compared to a metaphorical retreat in a natural surrounding with no creature comforts like electricity, a bathroom, television, or radio. To start with, Bride learns, most importantly, that materialism and craving are seeds not to be watered. Instead, essential values like generosity and nonjudgment must be cultivated: "It was too hard, too strange for her to understand the kind of care they offered—free, without judgment or even a passing interest in who she was or where she was going" (90). Morrison uses images and vocabulary that point to the idea of rebirth; the couple's house was deeply dark at night and "felt to Bride like being in a coffin" (92); there are several allusions to Bride's limping or inability to walk after the accident; thus, she resembles a baby or newborn. During her period of rest, Bride becomes more and more aware of what is essential in life and of what disinterested true love is. As she is reminded by Evelyn, money did not "save your ass" (91).

Another key element of mindfulness that dominates this six-week improvised retreat is, again, silence. And silence encourages self-awareness and understanding: "She was stuck in a place so primitive it didn't even have a radio. [. . .] There was no one to talk to, at least not about anything she was interested in" (98). It is worth noting the relevance of the number six as a symbol of equilibrium, health, and harmony (Cooper 116). The number six also signals a "turning point of a significant shift" and that "you are about to step into something new" (Dillard 264). Indeed, those six weeks represent a vital watershed in Bride's life.

Rain, the girl who appears after Bride's car crash, like the cleansing, purifying rain sent from heaven, will be a determinant factor in the protagonist's healing. This character's story awakens Bride into a different personal dimension, one of caring, selflessness, compassion, generosity, and, ultimately, understanding. The first time Rain and Bride actually talk follows a symbolic time of mindful silent walking together: "The quiet between them was easy at first as each appeared to be deep in her own thoughts. Bride limping, Rain skipping or dawdling along the verge of bushes and grass. Half a mile down the road Rain's husky voice broke the silence" (100). The break in silence is followed by Rain's first-person telling of her own story, a painful one. Rejected by her mother and forced out of their house, Rain represents the quintessence of orphanhood. By mindfully listening to this story, Bride comes to an understanding that drives her transformation. To start with, she immediately compares this girl's story to her own and realizes that at least Sweetness had never thrown her out. While Rain tells her story, she looks for blueberries but finds bitter ones, "not the wild sweet stuff she expected" (101). The play on words here is highly effective. The berries are a metaphorical allusion to Sweetness, Bride's bitter mother, and implicitly establish a connection between both characters, Rain and Bride. And in an unconscious gesture of connection, the one she was never offered by her own mother, "Bride took Rain's hand and led her gently to the stone," and "[t]hey both sat down" (102). Bride is adamant that she will hear Rain's cruel life story, and this means she is ready to listen attentively. Bride's repetition of the words "Tell me" several times expresses her eagerness to listen, and it is this mindful listening that makes the feeling of connection grow even deeper: "Listening to this tough little girl who wasted no time on self-pity, she felt a companionship that was surprisingly free of envy. Like the closeness of schoolgirls" (103).

Although Rain could be seen as a minor character in this novel, she plays a crucial role in the development of the plot. Even the dual name of this character is loaded with signification and symbolism. On the one hand, rain is a universal symbol of life and renewal, as well as spiritual cleansing and purification (Cooper 136). Thus, the appearance of Rain in Bride's journey certainly contributes to her regeneration. Moreover, RAIN is an acronym widely used in mindfulness programs to put together the four main stages or steps toward self-awareness: Recognition, Acceptance, Interest (or Investigation), and Nurture (Brach, *True* 62). These are the stages Bride goes through in her path to healing.

On the other hand, the child's other name, Raisin, has likewise multiple associations. If we take into account that grapes are the traditional fruit of sexuality and that a raisin is a dry grape, we can conclude that the name Raisin befits a character who has never had her menstrual period but has experienced sexuality in a distorted, cruel manner. This character's life has been symbolically dull and devoid of any hopes or dreams. But raisins are also deeply associated with mindfulness, as they are used in one of the most popular and well-known mindfulness exercises to show the benefits of mindful eating.

Part of what we have explained about Bride holds true for her beloved Booker. He is another fragmented character in deep need of catharsis and healing, his past trauma being the violent and sexually stimulated murder of his child brother. Whereas Bride finds a kind of refuge in sex, drinking, and pills, Booker resorts to music and the language of sound to alleviate his pain. Since he "had no words to describe his feelings" (131) or his traumatic memories, he gives vent to inner expression through unpunctuated written texts like the ones that appear in the last part of the novel. As Van der Kolk contends, traumatic memories are disorganized and dissociated, that is, "not properly assembled," and there is also chronological disruption (193, 194). This is what those fragments written by Booker show: unpunctuated overlapping sentences that deal with his own thoughts about the consequences of racism, about Bride, about his dead brother, and about heartbreak. The lack of punctuation also gives the idea of improvisation and musical language. As a matter of fact, all those journal entries are rich in musical vocabulary and the names of many musical instruments (cello, banjo, tympani, oboe, clarinet, and fiddle). Music is for Booker "his language of memory" (173).

If Bride's unexpected retreat at the hippie couple's home proves a key event in her path to healing, it continues at Booker's old aunt Queen's home. Despite the couple's pain over Queen's burns and ensuing death, their stay ends up being highly redemptive for both. The reader immediately notes that Queen resembles the ancestor mother-wit figure that Morrison introduces in many of her novels. She lives "alone in the wilderness" (159); her home is also compared to "a witch's den" (145), and the food she prepares is described as "manna" (145). In speaking with both Bride and Booker, she becomes the final incentive they need to culminate the healing process. In Bride she instills courage when she advises her against running away: "What's the matter with you? ... You come all this way and just turn around and leave?" (152). And she makes Booker realize that the past must never be a burden that rules and determines the present. She teaches him to free himself from the traumatic past and hold fast to the present. Previously described as "the exception to what Booker thought was mindless rote" (117), Queen warns about the danger of not living focused in the present, which is possibly why she is grateful to "Sweet Jesus" for having given her "a forgetfulness blanket along with a little pillow of wisdom to comfort her in old age" (159). In this sense, Queen's advice is steeped in mindfulness, as is her saying, "Booker ain't going nowhere" (144). "Nowhere" encloses the essence of mindfulness: now and here.

After talking to Queen and after reading Booker's journal, Bride finally opens up and reveals her childhood lie to Booker: "I lied! I lied! I lied! She was innocent. I helped convict her but she didn't do any of that" (153). Reading Booker's writing, Bride finally experiences a kind of epiphany whereby she finally understands the "shallowness" of looks and skin color; and, most importantly, she clearly sees her own cowardice, her running away from herself, the lesson her mother had taught her and had "nailed to her spine to curve it" (151). So by telling the truth now she finally makes amends not only with others but mainly with herself. Significantly enough, after confronting and telling her truth, her body comes back to adult shape. Once she acknowledges the childhood evils she had faced, her bodily regression disappears, which is also a sign of the culmination of the healing journey and of Bride's rebirth: "Having confessed Lula Ann's sins she felt newly born. No longer forced to relive, no, outlive the disdain of her mother and the abandonment of her father" (162).

After the serious talk with Queen, Booker sits on the doorstep in silence. Once again, what Tara Brach describes as "the power of the pause" (*Radical* 60) is at work, and that silent pause brings about epiphanic understanding: "Queen's right, he thought. Except for Adam I don't know anything about love. [. . .] The first major disagreement we had, and I was gone. My only judge being Adam who, as Queen said, is probably weary of being my burden and my cross" (161). According to clinical professor of psychiatry and codirector of the UCLA Mindful Awareness Research Center, Daniel Siegel, "A number of studies suggest that when you bring something into awareness and describe it, you can move that previously negative energy—a draining thought or cognition—into a new form" (Siegel).

This is what Booker does when he reflects about himself, as seen in the above quotation.

Booker's and Bride's evolution culminates with their taking care of Queen at death's door. After her injuries in an accidental fire at home, the two characters focus on her well-being and her recovery, putting aside their own personal situation. Referring to this fact, Morrison herself has pointed out that "[o]nly caring unselfishly for somebody else would accomplish true maturity" (*Origin* 51). On several occasions the narrator describes this idea of generosity and selflessness at the end of the novel: "They worked together like a true couple, thinking not of themselves, but of helping somebody else" (167), and "their focus was on a third person they both loved" (172–73).

The recurring image of the quilt Morrison uses in several of her works appears again in this novel. And, as it happens in *Home*, it is a metaphor for the final putting together of the patches that compose fragmented characters. In one of the two chapters devoted to Sofia Huxley, the innocent ex-convict Bride accused, we can read, "When I tend to my patients ... in my mind I am putting the black girl back together, healing her, thanking her. For the release" (77). This idea of putting a person back together is metaphorically portrayed in Queen's quilt (145). Quilts have traditionally been made and used by the African American community and have likewise been employed in literature to signify the healing of fragmented characters. It is interesting to note here that even if the seams that link the patches of the quilt are visible, the implied idea does not change. As is done in another artistic manifestation, the Japanese Kintsugi ceramics, the visibility of the cracks in a broken object represents the acceptance and beauty of their very existence and how they add meaning to the whole. Cathy Rentzenbrink explains, "Rather than try to hide the cracks, the potter works with gold to show us that the breakage will always be there and has become an acknowledged—and beautiful— part of the object's history" (76).

Although racism surely scars minds and lives, it can also be fought against by the power of introspective silence that will release the true self, devoid of self-loathing, much like a "true note" that can finally break the silence and be reborn. In the end both Bride and Booker understand and learn that being released from the past—once it has been dealt with—and embracing a more generous approach to life is necessary in order to be anchored in the present and to turn trauma into awareness, forgiveness, and acceptance. Booker finally realizes that Adam's death should not fetter his present life anymore, and he also comes into mindful understanding, in the silence of his thoughts: "I risk nothing. I sit on a throne and identify signs of imperfection in others. [. . .] I write notes about the shortcomings of others. Easy. So easy. What about my own?" (160–61).

As this essay demonstrates, *God Help the Child* can be read as a literary manifestation of mindfulness. It is a novel about awareness, compassion, gratitude, generosity, love, and the cultivation of silence. Even the anger Sofia Huxley feels for having been unfairly accused turns into a feeling of gratitude and compassion toward her accuser, Bride: "Now I think of it, that black girl did do me a favor. Not the foolish one she had in mind, not the money she offered, but the gift that neither of us planned: the release of tears unshed for fifteen years. No more bottling up. No more filth. Now I am clean and able" (70).

God Help the Child is also about the power of choice. At one point Booker tells Bride that "racism is a choice" (143); another character, Brooklyn, says that "hitting the floor . . . requires a choice—lie there or bounce" (49); and from a mindful perspective, healing and happiness ultimately boil down to choice, too, a choice one makes through the first step of mindfulness, the recognition of the now and here. As Viktor Frankl says, "Everything can be taken from a man but one thing: the last of the human freedoms—to choose one's attitude in any given set of circumstances, to choose one's own way" (86). And choice is intimately connected to the concept of agency or, as Van der Kolk puts it, "owning your life" (95). But agency does not necessarily reside in movement or action. Agency can also be present in moments of pause, quiet and stillness. Journeys are necessary for the culmination of healing and transformation but equally necessary are the times when the traveller stops and sits down. Without the breaks and stops, the journey would not be possible. As a profoundly mindful writer, Toni Morrison employs another powerful image and metaphor in her writing—the bench. A bench not only functions as a means to commemorate the forgotten neglected protagonists of history—as The Bench By the Road Project does—but also as a place to sit in silence and simply be fully present.

When we reach the end of this novel, the question Booker had asked Brooklyn comes to mind as a proleptic lesson of mindfulness: "Are you sure you know what makes a garden grow?" " . . . dung" is Booker's own reply (59–60). Turning dung into nurturing gardens represents the power to redefine and redirect concepts, like trauma. As the Vietnamese monk and mindfulness expert Thich Nhat Hanh argues, "We have to learn the art of transforming compost into flowers" (*True Love* 68). And in order to do so there must be a need to go nowhere but inside the self, now and here.

Notes

1. Interestingly enough, one of the characters of *GHTC* repeats the same words Baby Suggs used. When Bride reproaches Booker for his leaving her without saying a word or giving an explanation, she demands, "*Now* I want that word. Whatever it is I want to *hear it. Now.*" (153; my emphasis).

2. Two more examples can be seen in Milkman Dead's trip to the South in *Song of Solomon* under the ancestral guidance of both Pilate and Circe, and Frank Money's journey to rural Lotus in *Home* and the crucial presence of Miss Ethel in the healing of two characters, Frank and his sister Cee.

Works Cited

Brach, Tara. *Radical Acceptance: Awakening the Love That Heals Fear and Shame.* Rider, 2003.

———. *True Refuge: Finding Peace and Freedom in Your Own Awakened Heart.* Bantam, 2012.

Cooper, J. C. *An Illustrated Encyclopedia of Traditional Symbols.* Thames and Hudson, 1978.

Denard, Carolyn. "'Some to Hold, Some to Tell': Secrets and the Trope of Silence in *Love*." *Toni Morrison: Paradise, Love, A Mercy*, edited by Lucille P. Fultz, 77–91. Bloomsbury, 2013.

———, ed. Toni Morrison. *What Moves at the Margin: Selected Nonfiction.* UP of Mississippi, 2008.

Dillard, Sherrie. *Sacred Signs and Symbols: Awaken to the Messages and Synchronicities That Surround You.* St. Paul: Llewellyn, 2017.

Frankl, Viktor. *Man's Search for Meaning*. Washington Square Press, 1959.
Kabat-Zinn, Jon. Interview. *Mindful Magazine*. February 28, 2011. Accessed 2 February 2018. https://www.mindful.org/the-healing-power-of-mindfulness/.
Manyika, Sarah Ladipo. "On Meeting Toni Morrison." *Transition*, no. 124, Writing Black Canadas (2017), pp. 138–47.
Morrison, Toni. *Beloved*. Plume, 1987.
———. *The Bluest Eye*. New York: Holt, Rinehart, and Winston, 1970.
———. "The Dancing Mind." Carolyn Denard, ed. *Toni Morrison: What Moves at the Margin: Selected Nonfiction*. UP of Mississippi, 2008, pp. 187–90.
———. *God Help the Child*. Alfred A. Knopf, 2015.
———. *Home*. Knopf, 2012.
———. *The Origin of Others*. Cambridge: Harvard UP, 2017.
———. Remarks Given at the Howard University Charter Day Convocation. In Carolyn Denard, ed. *Toni Morrison: What Moves at the Margin: Selected Nonfiction*. UP of Mississippi, 2008, 164–69.
———. *Song of Solomon*. Knopf, 1977.
———. *Tar Baby*. Plume-Dutton, 1982.
Nhat Hanh, Thich. *Silence: The Power of Quiet in a World Full of Noise*. Rider, 2015.
———. *True Love: A Practice for Awakening the Heart*. Shambhala, 2004.
Rentzenbrink, Cathy. *A Manual for Heartache*. Picador, 2017.
Siegel, Daniel. *Mindful Magazine*. February 28, 2011. Accessed 2 February 2018. https://www.mindful.org/the-healing-power-of-mindfulness/.
Thurman, Robert. *The Contemplative Mind in Society*. Meeting of the working group September 29–October 2, 1994, Pocantico, NY. http://www.contemplativemind.org/files/thurman.pdf (Accessed on 2 February 2018).
Van der Kolk, Bessel A. *The Body Keeps the Score: Brain, Mind, and Body in the Healing of Trauma*. Penguin, 2014.
Walker, Kara. *Review of God Help The Child*. New York Times April 13, 2015.

Section 2

Subverting Whiteness: Writing beyond the Racialized Gaze

"What Did I Do to Be so Black and Blue?": Synesthesia in *God Help the Child*

Anissa Wardi

Toni Morrison's *God Help the Child* is a sparse novel. Readers accustomed to Morrison's epic works—such as *Song of Solomon*, *Beloved*, and *Paradise*—may find her last novel lacking. It is understandable that some readers yearn for a richer plot line, fleshed-out backstories, and greater character depth. Review after review addresses these issues: Kara Walker in the *New York Times* characterizes the novel as a "curt fable" replete with "clipped first-person confessionals." Roxane Gay, writing for the *Guardian*, maintains, "*God Help the Child* is the kind of novel where you can feel the magnificence just beyond your reach. The writing and storytelling are utterly compelling, but so much is frustratingly flawed. The story carries the shape of a far grander book, where the characters are more fully explored and there is far more at stake." "Never averse to risk," Donna Rifkind in the *Christian Science Monitor* writes, "Morrison strips this narrative of much of the temporal detail that tethered readers to the specific times and places of such books as 'Sula,' 'Beloved,' and 'Home' and rushes unencumbered into the storm." Finally, Saeed Jones, writing for NPR, turns to the language of aurality to convey the sparsity of Morrison's novel: "The music of Morrison's writing has been turned down so low, one is tempted to put their ear against the novel's pages." Though the responses to this slim novel range from praise to disappointment, Morrison does not shy away from her minimalist style, evidenced by Knopf's packaging of *God Help the Child*: the first words on the book jacket are "spare and unsparing." In a 2017 interview, Morrison shed light on her craft: "Some writers whom I admire say everything.

I have been more impressed with myself when I can say more with less instead of overdoing it, and making sure the reader knows every little detail. I'd like to rely more heavily on the reader's own emotions and intelligence" ("Write, Erase, Do it Over").

In that spirit, Walton Muyumba's review in the *Atlantic* offers an eloquent appraisal of the novel in light of Morrison's recent literary offerings: "Since *Love* (2003), Morrison has been working in what one might call her late style. Rather than craft big novels like *Tar Baby* or *Paradise*, she's distilled her fictions to their atomic elements. Morrison has chiseled and sculpted powerful narrative voices to drive these shorter, compressed works, each one paced for speed." My reading of *God Help the Child* is in line with Muyumba's. What I want to argue is that Morrison's lean art of storytelling in *God Help the Child* is evocative of a synesthetic experience whereby the reader, bereft of a richly developed narrative, is instead presented with a layered sensory experience of story and color. This is not to suggest that any one character in the novel is a synesthete; rather, Morrison's handling of color offers a distilled, yet cross-sensory vision of pain and trauma saturated with chromatic pigmentation. I am not the first to read a work of art through the lens of synesthesia. Janet Banfield argues: "We can think about artistic and other cultural practices in synaesthetic terms, and that in doing so, we are better placed to appreciate the ways in which these practices already do think with far more of our bodies than we customarily assume" (360).

The term "synesthesia" is defined as a union of the senses. It is a neurological condition in which the five senses are not locked into their separate channels but are intertwined in any number of ways. There are many forms of synesthesia; some estimates suggest that there "appear to be 80 varieties of these involuntary sensory perceptions" (Urist). Grapheme-Color Synesthesia, the term that refers to letter-to-color cross-talk, is, according to Gebuis, Nijboer, and van der Smagt, one of the most common synesthetic varieties. If we broaden grapheme-color synesthesia to consider language-to-color cross-modality, it affords a particularly apt lens for reading *God Help the Child*, insofar as Morrison relies heavily on articulating pain through color. Synesthesia is not a rare condition. Some estimate that one in two thousand people are synesthetes, while others argue that as many as one in three hundred have some variation of the condition. Notably, research shows that people with greater creative capacity are more likely to have synesthesia. Jacoba Urist in "Why Do So Many Artists Have Synesthesia?" reasons that "cross-sensory experiences may offer a particular artistic advantage: a greater aesthetic sensitivity than the rest of us, and thus a greater likelihood to gravitate toward artistic fields. After all, synesthetes are able to express seemingly unrelated concepts in a variety of mediums: number with personalities, colors with pain, moving shapes with sound.... An 'ordinary' painter either captures a landscape before her or something she imagines. A synesthetic one paints what she actually visualizes when hearing a specific concerto" (Urist). *God Help the Child*'s synesthetic qualities, and its cross-modal activation, create a world of pain and trauma that is saturated with pigment, in a sophisticated improvisation of narrative and color.

Morrison's push toward nonlinguistic literacy is in line with Susanne Langer in *Philosophy in a New Key*:

> I do believe that in this physical, space-time world of our experience there are things which do not fit the grammatical scheme of expression.... they are simply matters which require to be conceived through some symbolistic schema other than discursive language... the world of pure sensation is so complex, so fluid and full (71–72).

This fluidity of sensation is evocative of synesthesia. Joddy Murray offers a working definition of nondiscursive symbolization: it is "simply a term that accounts for the many other ways humans use symbols to create meaning—methods wholly outside the realm of traditional word-based discursive texts" (12). "Such symbolization," Murray explains, "includes art, but it also includes photographs, graphs, music, textile, ceramics, doodles, et cetera" (15). Langer's exploration of visual art is particularly useful in considering Morrison's project:

> Visual forms—lines, colors, proportions, etc.—are just as capable of articulation, i.e., of complex combination, as words. But the laws that

govern this sort of articulation are altogether different from the laws of syntax that govern language. The most radical difference is that visual forms are not discursive.... An idea that contains too many minute yet closely related parts, too many relations within relations, cannot be "projected" into discursive form; it is too subtle for speech. (78)

In *God Help the Child*, Morrison's work, though necessarily discursive, also moves into a nondiscursive realm, offering a sensory overlap between words and colors, articulating concepts that are "too subtle for speech." She asks her readers to participate in meaning-making, a kind of nonlinguistic literacy project that is primarily keyed to color. Morrison has repeatedly claimed that she is influenced by other aesthetic forms, including visual art and music. Most of her inspiration comes from African American art forms, including jazz, but, she explains, Edvard Munch's composition was seminal for her writing of a particular scene in *Song of Solomon*: "I was having some difficulty describing a scene in *Song of Solomon* ... of a man running away from some obligations and himself. I used an Edvard Munch painting almost literally. He is walking and there is nobody on his side of the street. Everybody is on the other side" ("Toni Morrison"). Thus, an attentive engagement to the visual and the aural allows for a deeper engagement with Morrison's artistry.

Child abuse is rampant in *God Help the Child*, but, arguably, two stories provide structure and depth to the narrative, namely, those of Lula Ann Bridewell and Booker Starbern. The novel chronicles, in brief, the life of Lula Ann, who as an adult changes her name to Bride. Sweetness, Bride's light-skinned mother, rejects her daughter just days after her birth when the baby's color begins to darken, claiming that "she was so black she scared me" (3); Bride's father, Louis, abandons the family because of his daughter's complexion. Sweetness is repelled by Bride, refuses to allow the child to call her Mama, and avoids physical contact with her daughter. In an attempt to curry her mother's affection, Bride joins with other children to falsely accuse an innocent teacher, Sofia Huxley, of child molestation, an act that lands the teacher in jail and haunts Bride throughout her life. Bride's story is paralleled to that of Booker, a man who becomes her lover. Booker's intact family is torn apart by the brutal rape, murder, and dismemberment of the eldest son, Adam. Booker, an intellectual and musician, is tormented by his brother's death and cannot, until the novel's end, convey this family tragedy to Bride; both struggle to find a language that adequately expresses their manifold traumas, which, this essay maintains, finds articulation through a rhetoric of color.

Morrison is an imaginative colorist, and thus *God Help the Child* is not the first time she has turned to the language of color. The author explored the chromatics of her work in the *Paris Review*, comparing the achromatic gray tones of *Beloved* to the brightly hued *Song of Solomon*:

> Part of that has to do with the visual images that I got being aware that in historical terms women, black people in general, were very attracted to very bright-colored clothing. Most people are frightened by color anyway. . . . They just are. In this culture quiet colors are considered elegant. Civilized Western people wouldn't buy blood-red sheets or dishes. There may be something more to it than what I am suggesting. But the slave population had no access even to what color there was, because they wore slave clothes, hand-me-downs, work clothes made out of burlap and sacking. For them a colored dress would be luxurious; it wouldn't matter whether it was rich or poor cloth . . . just to have a red or a yellow dress. I stripped *Beloved* of color so that there are only the small moments when Sethe runs amok buying ribbons and bows, enjoying herself the way children enjoy that kind of color. The whole business of color was why slavery was able to last such a long time. It wasn't as though you had a class of convicts who could dress themselves up and pass themselves off. No, these were people marked because of their skin color, as well as other features. So color is a signifying mark. ("Toni Morrison")

Here, Morrison's language moves effortlessly from color in the abstract to an exigency of chattel slavery and finally to skin color, and thus an attentive reading of color in Morrison's work is always already steeped in in a lexicon of race, offering a textured, multilayered presentation of chromatics. In the interview Morrison references Baby

Suggs, who, having lived through enslavement, freedom, the loss of all her children, and Sethe's infanticide of her granddaughter, spent her final years musing on color: "Her past had been like her present—intolerable—and since she knew death was anything but forgetfulness, she used the little energy left her for pondering color. 'Bring a little lavender in if you got any. Pink, if you don't.' And Sethe would oblige her with anything from fabric to her own tongue. Winter in Ohio was especially rough if you had an appetite for color" (*Beloved* 4). Perhaps, following Morrison's lead, we could surmise that Baby Suggs, multiply traumatized, relishes the beauty of the color spectrum before her death. Perhaps she chooses to dissolve into abstraction, anesthetize the pain that she had endured throughout her life, and let color usher her into death. Or perhaps Baby Suggs retreats into color not to forget, but to find a language to express what she had endured. In Morrison's oeuvre, color becomes an alternate signifying system. She employs the semantics of color when discursive language fails to render the enormity of a situation or the gravity of an emotional state. Color, in other words, steps in to do some of that work.

This argument is supported by Morrison's repeated commentary on language. With keen awareness of the limitations inherent in the medium in which she works, Morrison turns to the non-discursive symbol of color to signify outside of linguistic discourse. In her Nobel Lecture, for example, she claimed that "language can never pin down slavery, genocide or war. Nor should it yearn for the arrogance to do so. Its force, its felicity is in its reach toward the ineffable" (21). In *Beloved*, when the community of women gathers to vanquish the ghost that haunts 124 Bluestone Road, they perform a ritual that "broke the back of words," for "in the beginning," Morrison writes, "there were no words" (304). In *The Bluest Eye*, too, language fails Claudia. In her attempt to articulate the malignancy that is racism, Claudia turns to what is seemingly an empty signifier, "The *Thing* to fear was the *Thing* that made her beautiful, and not us" (74), in recognition that there can be no facile treatise on racism; such a far-reaching and ranging malevolence breaks the back of words.

In fact, a close attention to Morrison's literary enterprise suggests that the language of color is resplendent, perhaps as a reaction to the confines of linguistic codes. In her final novel, she takes this nondiscursive expression to the next level, boldly condensing the work to its basic elements, whittling down plot line to the point where narrative is delivered largely through colored elements. Using Morrison's language, I argue that *God Help the Child*, with its stark presentation of color, is her most painterly book.

Morrison's distilling process in *God Help the Child* is evocative of color field painting, a type of abstract expressionism pioneered in the late 1940s, which eschews figuration and even gestural abstraction in favor of color. In this style, "color is freed from objective context and becomes the subject in itself." Color field painting "abandoned all suggestions of figuration and instead exploited the expressive power of color by deploying it in large fields that might envelope the viewer when seen at close quarters" ("Color Field Painting").

That some color field artists present each painting as one unified, cohesive, monolithic image within a series of related types provides an interesting analogue to Morrison's newest project insofar as the resonant issue in *God Help the Child* is child abuse in its numerous forms. In giving voice and expression to the myriad of abuses catalogued in the text, Morrison allows color to deliver part of that narrative, and thus she is in line with color field pioneers, such as New York painter Helen Frankenthaler, who "diluted her paint, thinning it out so it melted into the weave of the canvas and became the canvas. And the canvas became the painting" (Stamberg). Color is the medium and the message: "these mega-size rectangles require letting your mind and eye leap right into the expanse of red, blue or green. Then you can almost feel the sensation of the colors themselves" ("Color Field Painting 101").

While Morrison's art, as a writer, cannot be reduced to color, it is the impulse to pare down her work and use color as an evocative signifying system, a kind of refining process, that is analogous to color field painters. Though Morrison's last novel is not grand in scale like many of the abstract expressionists, the depth of her color palette in *God Help the Child* likewise elicits a response from the readers whereby we "feel the sensation of the colors themselves." It is nearly impossible for readers to apprehend *God Help the Child* without being enveloped in Bride's blackness, a color that Morrison deftly describes as "blue-black," "Midnight black, Sudanese black" (3). Her darkness is alternately characterized in terms of food items, suggesting that blackness, a signifier of racial difference, is likewise a commodity to be consumed: Bride's skin is described as licorice, Hershey's syrup, and chocolate soufflé (33). In other words, Morrison conflates Bride with the color black, and thus readers, like the young child at the center of the novel, Rain, are forced to view her as the "black lady" (104). Bride's mother, Sweetness, is horrified by her daughter's skin color, calling her a "pickaninny" (5) and, for a brief moment, considering infanticide. She is embarrassed by her baby daughter and refuses to touch her tarlike skin (3), maintaining that "her color is a cross she will always carry" (7).

Despite the overwhelming blackness associated with Bride in the text, Morrison's chromatic presentation of the protagonist is, in fact, triadic. Bride's eyes are "crow black with a blue tint" (6). The mother labels her eyes "witchy" (6), and her friend describes them as "alien" (23). Here, readers of Morrison's fiction find yet another intertextual nod to *The Bluest Eye*; Pecola, the protagonist of Morrison's inaugural novel, yearns for blue eyes, a synecdoche for whiteness. Achieving, in part, the wished-for blue eyes that broke Pecola by the novel's end, Bride, read from a chromatic prism, is black and blue, a loaded racial color palette. Blue has long been used as a racialized descriptor. Since the fifteenth century, the term "blue blood" referred to skin that was so pale that blue veins could be seen through it, and was used as a marker of refinement. Blue bloods were often equated with aristocratic families and upper-class society; here, whiteness is a hierarchical marker of class and race. It should be noted that the ideology of African American intraracism also employed the discourse of blue bloods in the creation of Blue Vein Societies, in which lighter-skinner African Americans occupied positions of privilege. Interestingly, darker-hued African Americans are colloquially described as "blue-black," and in this way, the referent to blue in terms of epidermis is to both lightness and darkness.

The history of the color blue is likewise complex and contradictory. Tracing the color back to antiquity is complicated because, according to Philip Ball in *Bright Earth: The Invention of Color*, "it was not clearly recognized as a color in its own right.... It was regarded as a color related to black—a kind of gray" (233). To the Greeks, too, blue was a "species of darkness" (233). However, in the Middle Ages, blue, harvested from lapis lazuli, was the most prized color. It was expensive not only because it was imported from Afghanistan but because grinding the mineral into pigment was very labor-intensive. To use "ultramarine [a pigment made by grinding lapis lazuli into a powder] was not only to display one's wealth but—more important in the sacred works of the Middle Ages—to confer virtue in the painting. Nowhere is this more apparent than in the ubiquitous blue robe of the Virgin. To the monastic painter, the use of such materials conveyed due reverence" (239).

The color blue has strong cultural connotations of sadness in the West. As early as the fifteenth century, according to the *Oxford English Dictionary*, looking blue became a shorthand expression for showing melancholy, dejection, and sorrow. In the nineteenth century, there is a transmogrification from "looking" to "feeling" blue, yet the discourse of sadness aligned with the hue remained the same ("blue"). Perhaps painter Pablo Picasso best captured this chromatic association in what is famously known as his Blue Period, the period from 1901 to 1904 in which blue tones began to dominate his paintings: the "cool, bleak portraits of sick, hungry, aged, and poor [are] bathed in a blue glow" (Ball 231). This artistic outpouring was prompted by Picasso's depression following the suicide of his close friend and ended when his depression ceased.

The most resonant blue in *God Help the Child* is expressed through "the blues." Morrison signals the blues in the title of her novel, which is a take on one of Billie Holiday's signature songs.[2] Indeed, the novel traffics in the blues. Booker's home life is filled with music, "ragtime, old-time, jazzy records" (114), and Booker, who could not live without the music of Louis Armstrong, becomes, himself, a trumpet player. Booker briefly works as a music teacher, performs as a street musician, and creates a makeshift memorial service for his beloved aunt, scattering her ashes and playing "Kind of Blue."

Miles Davis's *Kind of Blue* is often cited as jazz's greatest record. In *Kind of Blue*, Davis experimented with modal jazz, "keeping the background of a tune simple while soloists played a melody over one or two 'modes,' or scales, instead of busy chord progressions—the usual harmonic foundation of jazz" (Luce). That musicians perform solos without distraction marks a clear analogy to the structure of *God Help the Child*. Morrison does not decorate these narratives but provides space for the characters' solos, as each sings his or her own blues. It is important to note that when Booker plays "Kind of Blue," it is "off-key and uninspired" (173). Believing that his musical performance had not expressed the proper respect for his aunt, Booker "cut it short and, with a sadness he had not felt since Adam's death, threw his trumpet in the gray water as though the trumpet had failed him rather than he had failed it" (173). While this gesture, born of grief, could signal the end of the blues in the novel, the blues aesthetic of Morrison's *God Help the Child* transcends Booker's artistry. In fact, the novel itself could be read as a blues melody and, in this way, offers another nondiscursive symbolic system. In graduate school Booker "began to shape unpunctuated sentences into musical language that expressed his questions about or results of his thinking" (122–23). Booker relied on this "soul-stretching music his father played . . . to oil and straighten his tangled feelings" (117). Delivering her narrative, in part, through chromatic and acoustic pain, Morrison presents chromesthesia, another synesthetic variety, characterized by sound-to-color cross-talk, which is perhaps best exemplified in the song "What Did I Do to Be So Black and Blue," a tune not directly referenced in *God Help the Child* but which could surely serve as its score. A Fats Waller song recorded many times by Louis Armstrong, "What Did I Do to Be So Black and Blue" is a treatise on racism and skin pigmentation translated through the language of color, mapped onto skin, and embodied in the blues tradition. Important to note for this analysis is the line "Because I'm black, I'm blue," referencing blackness as an always already part of the blues, a pairing that Morrison, too, highlights throughout the novel.

Bride's black and blue appearance is paired with white. Remaking herself into a cosmetics executive, Bride, on the advice of a stylist, clads herself exclusively in white: "You should always wear white, Bride. Only white and all white all the time. . . . Not only because of your name, but because of what it does to your licorice skin" (*God Help* 33). Bride remarks, "At first it was boring shopping for white-only clothes until I learned how many shades of white there were: ivory, oyster, alabaster, paper white, snow, cream, ecru, Champagne, ghost, bone" (33). Bride's stylist forbids her from wearing makeup: "Just you, girl. All sable and ice. A panther in snow. And with your body? And those wolverine eyes? Please!" 34). It is nearly impossible to read this treatise on black and white and not connect it to racial imagery. A dark-skinned woman highlights and accentuates her beauty by draping herself in white. Bride, later described as "spill of ink on white paper" 56), is reduced to a dyad of coloration. She is an embodiment of black and white (with a hint of blue). This interplay of color speaks to the phenomenon known as simultaneous contrast, which means that "a single color has the ability to shift and change depending on the color adjacent to it" (Eckstut and Eckstut 26). It can be argued, then, that Bride's blackness is perceived differently because it is always adjacent to whiteness. In this way Morrison offers a sophisticated color ontology imbued with racial implication.

In her description of Bride, Morrison nods to Frantz Fanon's *Black Skin, White Masks*. Fanon's groundbreaking work proposes a psychoanalytic reading of the colonized subject who, relentlessly imperiled by the colonial mind-set, imitates the culture of the colonizer and hence "wears the white mask." An adult Bride recalls the neighbor's condemnation of her skin color, casting her pigment as a mask or a heavy garment: "She's sort of pretty under all that black" (35). The painful recollection prompts Bride to self-soothe in a manner that symbolically replays this masking: "Besides, when I feel depressed the cure is tucked away in a little kit where his [Booker's] shaving equipment is. Lathering warm soapy water, I can hardly wait for the brushing and then the razor, the combination that both excites and soothes me. Lets me imagine without grief times when I was made fun of and hurt" 35). While Bride's secret ritual might be read as her attempt to hold on to Booker, or even as a moment of transgressive gender performance, given Morrison's detailed chromatic description of her shaving, it is most profitably read as Bride replaying her racialized trauma: "I use the dull edge and carve dark chocolate lanes through swirls of white lather" (35). Here, Bride is covering her blackness with whiteness, a pairing that sartorially (wearing all white) and discursively (shortening her name to "Bride") she enacts throughout her adult life.[3]

Abstract artist Sonia Delaunay, who worked with expressive color on textiles, argued that "the new art will really begin when we understand that colour has an existence of its own, that the infinite combinations of colours have a poetry and a poetic language much more expressive than anything before" (qtd. in Ball 301). Further, "Matisse felt, like Cezanne, that it is the relationship between the colors and not the forms of a painting that give it its structure" (Ball 303). Read from this prism, it is the interplay of black, white, and blue, and the attendant racial and cultural valences it carries, that embodies, in part, the novel's essence.

Morrison, employing an experience of complex synesthesia, intensifies perception and reconnects language to our color-saturated world. The chromatic harmony of black, white, and the cool shades of blue are juxtaposed with an expression of light. Morrison employs a yellow glow to illuminate the bright life of Adam, Booker's older brother. Adam, whom Booker adored, becomes a victim of a pedophiliac serial killer. Morrison again employs a nondiscursive system to capture Booker's final memory of Adam: "The last time Booker saw Adam he was skateboarding down the sidewalk in twilight, his yellow T-shirt fluorescent under the Northern Ash trees.... Down the sidewalk between hedges and towering trees Adam floated, a spot of gold down a shadowy tunnel toward the mouth of a living sun" (*God Help* 115). Booker's memory of Adam's luminosity does not fade even after Booker identifies his brother's body at the morgue: "unable to forget that final glow of yellow tunneling down the street, Booker placed a single yellow rose on the coffin lid and another, later, graveside" (116). In an attempt to capture and hold on to the light that is Adam, Booker inscribes his skin with color: "The tattoo artist didn't have the dazzling yellow of Booker's memory, so they settled for an orangish kind of red" (120–21).[4] Here, skin, a loaded signifier, takes on multilayered meanings. Beyond Booker's skin pigmentation, he marks his body with a luminescence that is concomitantly the color of loss.

Though Booker cannot capture the light, it is, ironically, only the light that makes seeing color possible. As Joann and Arielle Eckstut explain in *The Secret Language of Color*: "We happen to live on a planet bathed in sunlight. Because of this sunlight we, and many of our fellow living things, evolved to see color" (9). The authors further explain that "wavelengths of light do not exist as color until we see them. Without the eyes and brain, there's no such thing as color. Light waves are colorless until the moment they hit our eyes, at which point our brains declare, 'Blue sky, green grass, red rose!'" (20). So, seeing color is both neurological and cultural. We cannot see or assign meaning to color outside of our cultural norms, or, as Ball maintains: "The language of color reveals much about the way we conceptualize the world" (15). In recognition that color is a map of our perceptions, Morrison highlights the ways in which color in the abstract is always tied to skin melanin and all that the pigments carry in terms of racial hierarchy. Booker tries to locate the light and imprint it onto his skin only to realize that Adam's light (a kaleidoscope of clothing, setting sun, and spirit) is elusive; it is impossible to replicate such luminescence.[5]

Booker's memory is of Adam bathed in twilight, a mystical time between light and darkness. "At twilight shapes assume their softer, pastel forms. Things that were hard and definite again become soft, transient, and sublime. For a precious moment, all Earth glows. And then, in a moment just as precious, all sights disappear" (*National Geographic* 305). It is perhaps because light is still shining, a glow before darkness threatens to envelop the world, that we regard this liminal time as ethereal and spectral. For Booker, this moment captures not only the light before the night but life on the precipice of death. By the novel's end, he accepts the loss of his older brother; on the advice of his aunt, he no longer carries Adam, and the related inexpressible pain, on his back but finally allows him to rest, in a burial that, like his life, is mediated through dusk. Booker writes a kind of stream-of-consciousness farewell letter to Adam: "I don't miss you anymore adam rather i miss the emotion that your dying produced a feeling so strong it defined me while it erased you leaving only your absence for me to live in like the silence of the japanese gong that is more thrilling than whatever sound may follow" (*God Help* 161).[6] The letter finished, "[d]usk enveloped him and he let the warm air calm him while he looked forward to the dawn" (161). While the novel does not traffic in easy closures, for Booker, there is dawn, a time of new beginnings, a threshold that also holds personal meaning for Morrison herself.

Morrison discusses the ritual of her artistic process through the valences of color and light: "I always get up and make a cup of coffee while it is still dark—it must be dark—and then I drink the coffee and watch the light come.... For me, light is the signal in the transition. It's not being in the light, it's being there before it arrives. It enables me, in some sense" ("Toni Morrison"). In National Geographic Dawn to Dark Photographs, photographers for the society explain the beauty of this liminal time: "We both love to shoot in the early morning, before sunrise, as well as at dusk, after the sun has set. This is called the 'blue hour,' where you can capture a variety of mixed lights and moods" (42). Before sunlight illuminates our multihued landscape, the predawn realm seems awash in monochromatic shades. Yet, from a photographic perspective, this dreamlike world is bathed in blues; thus, Morrison, implicitly, begins her artistry on a blues note. Photojournalist Jim Richardson's musing on daybreak—"light races across the land in the morning. It will not wait" (*National Geographic* 135)— provides a context for Morrison's insistence that she bear witness to the end of night. Morrison, awake at first light, holds on to that brief space of shadows and dawn, an offering of luminosity and chromatic vision that finds manifold expression throughout her work. While black, blue, and white dominate the optic field of *God Help the Child*, Morrison intensifies the visual sensation of her color palette with the evanescence of light.

Morrison has remarked on numerous occasions that she wrote *The Bluest Eye* because she wanted to read it. What I want to suggest is that Morrison appears to have ceased writing novels *she* needs to read; instead, she writes open-ended stories that her *readers* need to read. Rather than dismissing Morrison's later style because it diverges from the intricate and detailed narratives of her early career, we—scholars, critics, and readers—would do well to consider the politics of Morrison's recent craft. Morrison offers readers a cross-sensory experience by readily employing various types of linguistic and nonlinguistic discourses. This synesthetic style allows readers to more readily write themselves into the story in what should be understood as Morrison's generous offer of textual cocreation. Reminiscent of Paul D's final thoughts to Sethe in *Beloved*—"He wants to put his story next to hers" (273)—Morrison's minimalistic style is an invitation for readers to put their stories next to hers.[7] After all, the dedication of *God Help the Child* is "For You."

Notes

1. Artistry and color figure in other Morrison novels as well. In *Sula*, for example, Morrison casts Sula in the role of an artist who is frustrated and destructive because she is bereft of a medium. In *Home*, Frank "Smart Money," a returning war veteran suffering from amnesia, sees the world in black and white: "Frank watched the flowers at the hem of her skirt blackening and her red blouse draining of color until it was white as milk. Then everybody, everything.... All color disappeared and the world became a black-and-white movie screen" (25). As he begins to heal, his sense of color returns. Likewise, his sister Cee's physical healing is associated with pigmentation: she creates a quilt of "lilac, crimson, yellow, and dark navy blue" (143).

2. Interestingly, Holiday, in her autobiography, *Lady Sings the Blues*, wrote about her difficult childhood.

3. In "What Did I Do to Be So Black and Blue?" Waller also speaks to masking: "I'm white inside, it don't help my case, 'Cause I can't hide what is on my face." Here, the masking takes on a crucial difference. Rather than adopt Eurocentric attributes (and wear the white mask), the speaker, it seems, suggests that he is as worthy and important as whites but is deemed inferior. I don't believe that the speaker prizes whiteness; rather, he provides a social commentary through the discourse of color.

4. The fact that Booker could not find a color that matches the fading radiance of the sun is in line with many visual artists who claim that synthetic paints are incapable of capturing the depth and breadth of our multihued natural world. Mycologist and botanical illustrator Mary Banning, for example, in referencing the glowing colors of fungi, remarked: "I invite the careful observation of the skeptical and they will find that their paint boxes hardly afford pigments bright enough to sketch those beauties of the woods" (qtd. in Eckstut and Eckstut 139).

5. That Morrison illustrates Adam's life force through light echoes the philosophy of Greek Orthodoxy, which "emphasizes the light inside every human being and so icon paintings also begin with light, which seems to shine through the pigments and through the gold laid on top" (Finlay 23).

6. In Morrison's hands, silence is not an absence but is, itself, a language. Since Adam's death, Booker has lived in the silence that followed that defining sound.

7. Morrison has remarked that she purposefully leaves holes and gaps in her novels, so that the reader can find a place to come in. While she has played with this narrative style throughout her literary career, it is more pronounced in her later works. As readers, we may still yearn for Milkman's soaring flight, but instead, using Morrison's words on jazz music, we are left at the precipice with no satisfying conclusion: "Jazz always keeps you on the edge. There is no final chord. There may be a long chord, but no final chord.... I want my books to be like that—because I want that feeling of something held in reserve and the sense that there is something more" ("Interview with Toni Morrison" 411).

Works Cited

Ball, Phillip. *Bright Earth: Art and the Invention of Color*. U of Chicago P, 2003.
Banfield, Janet. "'A Sprinkling of Sugar Dust': Synaesthetic Practices, Affective Entertainment, and Non-Representational Communication." *Cultural Geographies*, vol. 23, no. 2, 2016, pp. 357–61.
"blue." OED Online. Oxford University Press, 25 March 2017.
"Color Field Painting." *The Art Story*. The Art Story Foundation, n.d. Accessed 17 Mar. 2017.
"Color Field Painting 101." Ms. Chang's Art Classes. n.d. Accessed 30 Jan. 2017.
Eckstut, Joann, and Arielle Eckstut. *The Secret Language of Color: Science, Nature, History, Culture, Beauty of Red, Orange, Yellow, Green, Blue & Violet*. Black Dog and Leventhal, 2013.
Fanon, Frantz. *Black Skin, White Masks*. Grove, 1967.
Finlay, Victoria. *Color: A Natural History of the Palette*. Random House, 2002.
Gay, Roxane. "God Help the Child by Toni Morrison Review – 'Incredibly Powerful.'" *Guardian*. Guardian News and Media, 29 Apr. 2015. Accessed 14 Mar. 2017.
Gebuis, Titia, Tanja C. Nijober, and Maarten J. van der Smagt. "Of Colored Numbers and Numbered Colors: Interactive Processes in Grapheme-Color Synesthesia." *Experimental Psychology*, vol. 56, no. 3, 2009, pp. 180–87.
"Jazz Profiles from NPR: Miles Davis' *Kind of Blue*." NPR, n.d. Accessed 17 March 2017.
Jones, Saeed. "Toni Morrison's New Novel Is Best Read with Her Backlist in Mind." NPR. 22 Apr. 2015. Accessed 14 Mar. 2017.
Langer, Susanne. *Philosophy in a New Key*. New American Library, 1969.
Luce, Jim. "Jazz Profiles from NPR Miles Davis: Kind of Blue." *NPR*. n.d. Accessed 17 Mar. 2017.
Morrison, Toni. *Beloved*. Plume, 1987.
———. *The Bluest Eye*. 1970. Plume, 1993.
———. *God Help the Child*. Knopf, 2015.
———. "An Interview with Toni Morrison." Interview by Nellie McKay. *Toni Morrison: Critical Perspectives Past and Present*, edited by Henry Louis Gates Jr. and K. A. Appiah. Amistad, 1993, pp. 396–411.

———. *The Nobel Lecture in Literature*, 1993. Knopf, 1994.

———. *Song of Solomon*. Penguin, 1977.

———. "Toni Morrison, The Art of Fiction No. 134." Interview by Elissa Schappell. *Paris Review* 1993: n. pag. Accessed 17 Mar. 2017.

———. "Write, Erase, Do It Over." Interview by Rebecca Gross. *NEA Arts Magazine*. n.d. Accessed 14 Mar. 2017. https://www.arts.gov/NEARTS/2014v4-art-failure-importance-risk-and-experimentation/toni-morrison.

Murray, Joddy. *Non-discursive Rhetoric: Image and Affect in Multimodal Composition*. State U of New York P, 2009.

Muyumba, Walton. "Lady Sings the Blues." *Atlantic*. Atlantic Media Company, 23 Apr. 2015. Accessed 14 Mar. 2017.

National Geographic Dawn to Dark Photographs: The Magic of Light. National Geographic Society, 2015.

Rifkind, Donna. "'God Help the Child' Is Toni Morrison's Latest Exploration of the Hurt That Drives Us." *Christian Science Monitor*. 4 May 2015. Accessed 14 Mar. 2017.

Stamberg, Susan. "'Color Field' Artists Found a Different Way." *NPR*. 4 Mar. 2008. Accessed 17 Mar. 2017.

Urist, Jacoba. "Why Do So Many Artists Have Synesthesia?" *Science of Us*. New York Media, 7 July 2016. Accessed 14 Mar. 2017.

Walker, Kara. "Toni Morrison's 'God Help the Child.'" *New York Times*. 13 Apr. 2015. Accessed 14 Mar. 2017.

Waller, Fats. "What Did I Do to Be So Black and Blue?" 1929. Accessed 17 Mar. 2017.

"You Not the Woman I Want": Toni Morrison's *God Help the Child* and the Legend of Galatea

Maxine Lavon Montgomery

> *But there is culture and both gender and "race" inform and are informed by it. African American culture exists and though it is clear (and becoming clearer) how it has responded to Western culture, the instances where and means by which it has shaped Western culture are poorly recognized or understood.*
> Toni Morrison, "Unspeakable Things Unspoken"

In a scene that could have appeared in a gothic romance novel, Booker Starbern, a free-spirited trumpeter, tells his lover, Lula Ann Bridewell, "You not the woman I want."[1] Booker delivers the stinging rebuff after learning of Bride's attempt to reach out to an alleged child molester. Not only do his comments set the stage for the baffling physical transformation that the young woman undergoes when she returns to a prepubescent state, they also serve as a catalyst for Bride's self-reflexive search for her estranged lover. The star-crossed couple have a chaotic relationship punctuated by moments of passionate sex, bouts of violence, and eventual reconciliation as they anticipate the birth of their first child. Morrison relies upon a range of antecedent sources in her representation of the couple's tumultuous bond. Chief among those influences is Greco-Roman myth with the account of Galatea, an animated statue that comes to life as a result of the careful sculpting on the part of Pygmalion.

Morrison's eleventh and final novel, *God Help the Child*, originally titled *The Wrath of the Children*, is an intriguing, multilayered work of fiction echoing myth, biblical lore, and the fairy tale, but without the simplistic resolution often attributed to the fable.[2] As with her earlier texts, there are no happy endings or neat resolutions to the vexed issues Morrison engages. Booker and Bride's six-month romance comes to an abrupt end once he learns of her conciliatory gestures in reaching out to an assumed child abuser; the trumpeter makes an uneasy truce with his family following the tragic death of his older brother; and the novel closes with the haunting voice of Sweetness, Bride's estranged mother, who expresses guarded optimism at the prospect of the couple's moving forward in light of the challenges that lie ahead. The rather slim novella is as invested in dismantling utopian notions of life in twenty-first-century America as it is in revealing the trauma associated with childhood sexual abuse.

Ovid's epic poem *Metamorphoses* offers a likely classical backdrop for the contemporary tale of the journey toward wholeness on the part of Booker and Bride, two ill-fated lovers who must come to terms with a troubled past that refuses to release its stranglehold on the present. Bride's erasure and restoration finds an ancient analogue in Galatea's transmutation from artifact to enlivened persona. Morrison readily acknowledges her indebtedness to the Greco-Roman tradition in ways that underscore her reluctance to formulate a clear distinction between the classics, which she rightly associates with a European heritage embedded in an ideological whiteness, and black vernacular communal structures.[3] Tessa Roynon makes a persuasive case for the close, conversational relationship between Morrison's evolving canon and the classical tradition of Homer, Aeschylus, Euripides, Virgil, and Ovid (*Toni Morrison and the Classical Tradition*, 2014). Roynon demonstrates that Morrison's classicism is fundamental to the author's revisionist technique and the critique of American and Western culture. The award-winning author refuses to acknowledge a construction of black culture that would separate it from the classics; nor is she willing to ascribe authority to the Greco-Roman tradition in ways that would suggest its preeminence in hierarchal fashion over raced and gendered forms.

This ambiguity is impressively at work in Morrison's final work of fiction as the author situates her text within a tradition of black women authors who investigate gendered and racial decodings of black women in literature and offer what Mae Gwendolyn Henderson describes as "strong revisionary methods of reading, focusing as they do on literary discourses regarded as marginal to the dominant literary-critical tradition" (349). Morrison's reading of classical tales involves disruption and revision. "Disruption—the initial response to hegemonic and ambiguously (non)hegemonic discourse—and revision (rewriting or rereading)," Henderson points out, "together suggest a model for reading black and female literary expression" (358). My aim is not to belabor the conversation surrounding Morrison's signifying engagement with the classical tradition but to interrogate her narrative and rhetorical method in talking back to Ovid in *God Help the Child*. She reinscribes the trope of the animated statue using a synergistic strategy resonant with storytelling and invested in a Diaspora imaginary involving slavery, the Middle Passage, and colonization—key events defining a specifically raced, transnational history.

The legend of the enigmatic Galatea lends itself well to the creative reinvention at the center of Morrison's text. In an account that privileges a masculinist artistic enterprise, Pygmalion sculpts Galatea out of ivory in order to fashion his ideal woman—a figure who undergoes multiple reconstructions before she conforms to his romanticized conception of feminine attractiveness.[4] With the assistance of Aphrodite, goddess of love, beauty, and sexuality, Galatea comes to life. Pygmalion then falls in love with his statue, forsakes bachelorhood, and embraces matrimonial bliss as Aphrodite rewards the couple with the birth of a child. Galatea's role also involves her figuration as a sea nymph, depicted in Homer's *Odyssey* as a beautiful woman riding side-saddle upon the back of a fish-tailed god. The alluring sea goddess enchants the musician Polyphemus, who woos her with tunes from his pipes.

Rather than merely extending the narrative world of the classics, Morrison upsets the identity politics undergirding Greco-Roman stories by endowing the principal female persona with the voice, agency, and subjectivity denied to her in the earlier accounts. Morrison adopts a similar strategy in revoicing the servant girl, Barbary, in *Desdemona*, a cover version of Shakespeare's *Othello*. Bride, a beautiful cosmetics executive, tells a story of childhood abuse, ridicule, and trauma rooted in a conflicted relationship with her mother. Sweetness, Bride's light-skinned mother, rejects the dark-skinned daughter out of a deference to "skin privileges" and withholds the maternal affection that Bride craves (43). Assuming that his wife is guilty of an adulterous affair, Bride's father abandons the family, leaving Sweetness to raise her daughter alone.

Sweetness is the last in a succession of guilt-ridden mothers in Morrison's oeuvre, including Pauline Breedlove, Eva Peace, Sethe, and the nameless mother whose poignant story bookends *A Mercy*. Like *A Mercy*'s Minha Mae, Sweetness hovers ominously over the novel in ghostlike fashion, interrupting the interlocking stories that Bride, Booker, Brooklyn, Sofia, and Rain relate. Throughout the novel, Sweetness remains invisible, largely nameless, a ghostly figure embedded in the daughter's memorial structures, as befits the mother's partially symbolic role as a figure for Mother Africa, a diasporic home that is neither immediately accessible to nor completely removed from the postslavery subject. Yet Sweetness, too, has a voice and speaks to the reader from the unexplored margins of a diasporic geography. Morrison's decision to revoice the dispossessed black female subject, along with her efforts to situate narrative action involving Bride's search for Booker within a discursive nexus involving the conflicted mother-child dyad, directs attention to what she theorizes as the "dark, abiding signing Africanist presence" (*Playing in the Dark* 45). She argues that this presence is a result of white writers' inability to create race-free texts. That project is impossible, since Africans and African Americans are interwoven into the very fabric of American society and white American consciousness. Morrison's depiction of the nameless mother as a symbolic figure also foregrounds issues relevant to identity, representation, and genealogical origins at the center of black women's literary and cultural production. By turning the faint notion of Africa into a reality, Morrison addresses her fraught relationship with canonical authors while rewriting the forgotten moments marking the black experience in a New World setting.

Morrison's use of the rejected child as a significant persona summons the specter of diasporic beginnings that predate colonial inscriptions of time, space, and identity. The novel's landscape is thus strewn with an assortment of abandoned/orphaned/rejected children, each one, like the scarred Galatea, bearing the physical, emotional, and psychological marks of a chaotic history. Bride is disfigured as a result of Sofia Huxley's brutal attack. Booker, who distances himself from his family when they fail to exhibit compassion after the disappearance of Adam, is given to bouts of rage because of unresolved grief. Rain, the mysterious orphan who befriends Bride, longs for family and home. Sofia, who is at odds with her abusive, fanatically religious mother, attempts to atone for the past through her healing gestures at a nursing home. Brooklyn continues to suffer as a result of her mother's failure to protect the daughter from an uncle's sexual exploitation. Queen has lingering guilt because of her refusal to believe Hannah's reports of sexual misuse.

That the mother in her myriad guises is not specifically raced points to Morrison's efforts to trouble representations of the mother figure rooted in an essentialist identity construct and to question utopian depictions of a Mother Country that welcomes immigrants with open arms (Valkeakari). Morrison's reliance upon a global assembly of storytellers therefore undermines the grand metanarrative of genealogy and influence serving as the impetus for notions of whiteness underlying popular constructions of a classical narrative tradition. Even though Brooklyn is "chalk white," she has blonde dreadlocked hair and dates black men (131). Mr. Leigh, the child-molesting landlord, is identified in terms of his "hairy white thighs" (54). The emerald-eyed Rain is racially ambiguous. There is no mention of the racial identity of Sofia Huxley, the schoolteacher whom Bride wrongly accuses of molestation, although Sofia's fascination with Bride's dark complexion, which is prevalent among the female inmates at Decagon, suggests that Sofia is *not* black. For Sofia, blackness is the exception rather than the normative identity. Morrison remarks regarding the problematic issue of race in *God Help the Child* that "color is both a curse and a blessing, a hammer and a golden ring" (*Origin of Others* 51). As she does in "Recitatif," *Paradise*, and, to a lesser degree, *A Mercy* and *Home*,

Morrison undermines reader expectation where identity is concerned by pairing racial markers with their opposites.

Morrison endeavors to undermine Ovid's authority, clapping back, as it were, to the famed canonical Greek author by reframing the trope of the animated ivory statue within a symbolic, intermediate space where identity is fluid, not fixed, and subjectivity is as indistinct as the vague postracial seaside California setting where the novel's action occurs. She pays particular attention not only to Bride and Booker but also to a range of multiracial subjects, giving voice to them in a way that Ovid, as a Greco-Roman poet, could not. At the discursive center of the novel is Bride's journey—with literal and symbolic overtones—through the labyrinth of contemporary America's cultural, social, and institutional life while the alluring twenty-three-year-old cosmetics executive moves from an objectified positioning to a reality that is more self-defined.

Like the adolescent Pecola Breedlove, Bride struggles with issues of self-hatred traceable to the politics of cultural representation embedded in a Fanonian lexicon of the gaze (Fanon 167). Beauty is coded as white within the dominant society, as is evident by Jeri's suggestion that Bride wear only white, in a performative way, a move that occasions the young executive's meteoric rise to prominence in her profession and adoration from colleagues, clients, and acquaintances. Bride's all-white attire also reifies the black-white binary resulting in a loss of self-identity. Unlike her fictional predecessor, Pecola, who is entrapped within the perimeters of "the look," however, Bride offers an example of spectacular blackness when the beautiful cosmetics executive promotes her raced identity—a fetishized self—for mass-market consumption: she drives a Jaguar, carries designer purses, wears expensive clothes, and, in a gesture that recalls the folkloric trickster story, dons rabbit-fur boots.

Booker's initial sighting of Bride is a transcendent moment couched in terms richly suggestive of a pre-colonial glance signifying the existence of a semidivine female ancestor. "Her clothes were white," Booker observes, "her hair like a million black butterflies asleep on her head" (130–31).[5] He sees Bride and Brooklyn exiting a limousine while he is en route to one of many street performances.

"When he stepped through that cloud and became as emotionally content as he had been before Adam skated into the sunset—there she was. A midnight Galatea always and already alive" (132). Booker's reference to the glamorous Bride as his "*midnight* Galatea" brings to mind Ovid's dynamic ivory statue, refigured as a specifically cultured persona who is a potential source of healing (emphasis added). The text thus seizes upon notions of "in-between-ness" associated with what Homi Bhabha aptly describes as the "post" as a locus for refiguring both the historical loss on the part of the postslavery, postracial subject and the insistent need for recovery of a vanished past linked inextricably with the feminine (43). Other scholars are more direct in making an association between this liminal space or metaphoric crossroads and the Middle Passage, a locus for cultural confluence and trans-national exchange (Gilroy, *Black Atlantic*, 1993; Wardi, *Water and African-American Memory* 2011; and Valkeakari, *Precarious Passages* 2017). They rightly assert that, rather than serving exclusively as places of tragedy, separation, death, and loss, diasporas can also function as fluid sites of convergence between nations, cultures, and worlds.

Booker's remarks upon his first sighting of Bride therefore reveal a conflation of the Ovidian statue, whose name means "she who is milk white," with a timeless, raced female figure whose presence is redemptive, restorative, and enabling. It is Bride who offers Booker temporary relief from the grief surrounding the deaths of Booker's twin, along with Adam, an Ur-self or original persona that reminds the reader of the viability of the unseen and the psychological wounds Booker carries. Whereas Morrison casts the sexually transgressive Sula into the role of frustrated artist, the author engages in what Judith Butler would describe as a gender-bending play by ascribing that designation to Booker, a besieged musician and writer whose artistic enterprises recall the masculinist creative endeavors of Pygmalion, Polyphemus, and, equally important, Ovid himself (*Gender Trouble* 1990). But Booker's talent as writer and musician is mediocre at best. Only with Bride's command does the musician realize the latent power of his artistic potential. Once he sees Bride his music takes on an uplifting quality. "What emerged was music he had never played before. Low, muted notes held long, too long, as the strains floated through drops of rain" (131). Booker's foray into writing also bears the marks of Bride's appeal, as he is able to "put on paper words he could not speak" (161).

As a struggling artist who settles for a job teaching music at a junior high school because of his unsuccessful music auditions, Booker learns that his gift is limited without Bride's muselike inspiring influence. She is the wellspring of his long-suppressed creativity. Yet in the fictional world that Morrison fashions, both male and female subjects evolve toward a self-defined position that exists outside the boundaries of constituted social categories. Narrative action therefore entails the journey on the part of Booker and Bride from an imprisonment within the pain of childhood trauma to a place where each is willing to embrace community. Here, the role ascribed to Galatea as not only an animated statue but an enchanting sea nymph is relevant in an appreciation of Morrison's use of a Diaspora imaginary in reinscribing classical myth. Water is a recurring trope throughout the novel. Bride notices the rain on the day following Booker's rebuff. The cosmetics executive wears a white lace gown with a mermaidlike flounce at her ankles (50). Booker first sees Bride during a torrential downpour. The couple spend countless hours at a seaside retreat. Evelyn and Steve find the mystifying girl, Rain, in the rain. The trumpeter steps out into a rainstorm after quarreling with his family over a fitting memorial to Adam. Booker resides "down the road, the last house beside the stream" (151). In *Water and African American Memory: An Eco-critical Perspective*, Anissa J. Wardi makes a convincing case for the role of water and bodies of water in terms of their spiritual, cultural, and political implications for black literature, film, and aspects of expressive culture. Particularly relevant to the present discussion is Wardi's assertion that "water is employed as a framework for theorizing survival and trauma, diasporic and regional connections, and physical and psychological dislocations" (3). Water, in all of its varied forms, in the black narrative serves as a powerfully evocative trope for the multidirectional journey on the part of a migratory subject. It reveals the persistence of, and inherent complications with, routes and roots—the individual and collective longing for a return to ancestral origins. Not surprisingly, then, Booker, a postracial representation of the male artist, discards his trumpet in the water at the novel's end. Like Polyphemus's reed pipe, Booker's beloved trumpet is as much a symbolic representation of his masculine identity as a signifier of his musical gift. Booker's act is thus a ritual gesture signaling at once both an awareness of a diasporic history resonant with the Middle Passage and a deference, long overdue, to the inspirational power of the feminine.

Booker's glowing assessment of Bride, who symbolizes what Morrison refers to as "an invisible mediating force," also brings to mind the Derridian notion of trace, or the always-already as a process that is perpetually in motion, waiting to be revealed or recognized (*Playing* 46–47). In deconstructionist theory, absent things leave traces of their presence, erasing, in a Derridian sense, the boundary between what is seen and unseen (12–16). "Trace can be seen as an always contingent term for a 'mark of the absence of a presence, an always-already absent present,' of 'the originary lack' that seems to be the condition of thought and experience" (Macksey and Donato 1970, 254). Similarly, Morrison gestures toward the symbolic associations of absence and presence in her remarks about the ancestor, "a timeless figure whose relations to the characters are benevolent, and protective, and they provide a certain kind of wisdom" ("Rootedness" 343). The author's reliance upon the ancestor or ghost as a sign or symbol, whose "curious dual force makes present what is absent," enables a recapitulation of the past in powerful ways (Brogan, 29; La Capra, 53, 68–69). Bride, an embodiment of the many problematical readings of a so-called authentic raced persona, is a figure allowing Morrison to critique a whitewashing of Western culture and the systematic erasure of the black subject. As a character closely aligned with a range of ambiguous female personae in Morrison's canon, including *Jazz*'s sexually transgressive Wild, *Love*'s ethereal sea goddess, Celestial, and the eponymous ghost-child, Beloved, Bride is thus not only someone who brings order and clarity into Booker's otherwise chaotic life; she is also associated with a preternatural realm existing apart from a colonizing influence.

The mark of the absence of a presence is evident throughout the novel, encouraging a critique of fixed identity constructs based upon Hegelian notions of a split between self and other, masculine and feminine, blackness and whiteness. In a similar sense, the space demarcating antecedent textual boundaries loses validity in the account of Bride's journey to Whiskey. Morrison's rendering of the trip to the agrarian community involves a destabilizing mash-up of classical myth, the fairy tale, and biblical tradition. Reminiscent of Milkman's passage to pastoral Shalimar in *Song of Solomon*, or Frank "Smart" Money's return to Lotus, Georgia, in *Home*, Bride's quest for her estranged lover, Booker, is a journey into the unknown. Her trek assumes epic dimensions with her trip, first to Steve and Evelyn's woodsy residence, and later her arrival in Whiskey, where she encounters Queen, Booker's forgetful but all-knowing aunt. The elder wise woman invites a comparison with Aphrodite in a particularly "Morrisonian" attempt to recuperate a buried history involving the exploits of a larger-than-life raced female personality. Aside from Bride's return to childhood, Queen's death as a result of her attempts to burn her mattress springs is perhaps the most improbable aspect of the novel. But like Aphrodite, whose fiery display presages Galatea's incarnation and Pygmalion's marriage to the animated statue, Queen is a timeless, benevolent ancestral figure.

Not only does Booker's aunt double as the legendary classical persona, she also reembodies the wicked stepmother of fairy tale renown.[6] Bride fears that she is "being seduced into a witch's den" as the young cosmetics executive conflates her uncertainty about Queen's motivations with the childhood abuse Bride suffers (145). When Bride arrives at Queen's residence, in what could be read as another erasure of identity, the young woman sees herself as a refiguration of Pecola Breedlove. Bride becomes "the ugly, too-black little girl in her mother's house" (144).

Queen is an ancestral figure whose mother-wit, knowledge of healing arts, cooking, and sewing represent a reconnection with an idealized rural home, a symbolic site where parts torn as a result of the trans-Atlantic journey are healed, in the terms that Evelyn Jaffe Schreiber sets forth (2010). But the account of the elder woman's multiple marriages to men representing a range of ethnicities complicates the portrait of the semidivine maternal persona figuring into texts by African American women along with the ostensibly seamless narrative involving the heroic route home on the part of the migratory subject. Queen leads Bride to a deeper comprehension of Booker's cryptic notes. Before Queen's death, Bride bathes Booker's aunt in an elaborate rite of cleansing, renewal, and baptism that Joann Gabbin would refer to as "a laying on of hands," a transcendent narrative moment outside a masculine, racialized gaze signaling a restored bond of sisterhood among dispossessed women across time and space (Braxton and McLaughlin). Queen conflates Bride with Hannah, the daughter Queen fails to protect from child abuse. Significantly, however, like the biblical Hannah who was, at first, barren, Bride prepares to enter motherhood at the novel's end, thereby signaling a possible restoration of the ruptured mother-child bond. Not surprisingly, when Queen learns of Bride's efforts to reconcile with Booker, the elder woman sings the classic tune "Stormy Weather," an oblique, bluesy signifying reference that summons at once both the uncertain perils of the turbulent Middle Passage and the future of the couple's unstable relationship.

It is during her trip to Whiskey that Bride learns the truth of Booker's past. With Queen's assistance the young woman also discovers that Booker's otherwise uninspired writing is "about me, not him. Me!" (152). Together, Booker and Bride progress from the one-dimensionality associated with an objectifying gaze to psychological complexity. Their progression parallels the willingness to put aside their self-centered concerns in order to align themselves with others. Morrison's comments shed light on the ways in which Booker and Bride elide the color fetish central to the American cultural mythos when the author points out, "Only caring unselfishly for somebody else would accomplish true maturity" (*Origin of Others* 51). Booker is therefore thrilled to find that Bride has evolved, as she has "changed from one dimension into three—demanding, perceptive, daring" (173). As if to signal the visual or "painterly" aesthetics associated with Morrison's "writerly" representation of the transformation from object to subject, from individuality to community, the novel moves from an emphasis on blackness and whiteness to an ekphrastic focus on a range of colors.[7] The highlighting of a multiplicity of colors following Bride and Booker's discovery of the hidden truths surrounding their respective pasts points to a multifaceted understanding of America that belies the apparent oppositional tension of Bride's early, raced perspective. This new awareness also signals Morrison's efforts to upend the identity politics undergirding representations of a snow-white Galatea in the classical imagination. Queen's mismatched quilt "pieced in soft colors" reveals the shift toward healing and recovery when Bride arrives at a more enlightened comprehension of self and society (145).

Bride's journey toward healing culminates with "the magical return of her flawless breasts," a symbol for maternity and fertility (167).[8] Booker's evolution is complete with his reluctant acknowledgment of the limitation of his artistic sensibility. "And what made him think he was a talented trumpet player who could do justice to a burial or that music could be his language of memory, of celebration or the displacement of loss" (174). In a ceremonial moment resonant with loss, mourning, and celebration, Booker delivers a final musical tribute to his deceased aunt as the newly reunited couple pay homage to the female ancestor. At the novel's end, Booker and Bride make a temporary truce with the ghosts of the past. The scene involving scattering Queen's ashes in the water reverberates with recollections of Diaspora. Although the anticipated birth of Booker and Bride's child points to a bright future, Sweetness's closing words lend a note of guarded optimism to the couple's plans. Reality will once again intrude on the couple's lives, despite the hopefulness that Booker and Bride express. The novel's ambiguous ending therefore returns the reader to an intermediate space outside of fixed cultural and geographic bounds.

Booker tells Bride, "You not the woman I want" (8). Equally as important to an understanding of their troubled relationship is her pointed response, "Neither am I" (8). Morrison constructs a three-dimensional, psychologically complex female subject who is capable of voicing her own story, and as much as any other text in the author's evolving canon, *God Help the Child* extends the scholarly conversation surrounding matters of race, identity, and representation in a New World setting, with classical masterpieces serving as a call prompting a uniquely 'Morrisonian' response. Her text functions as a site of resistance allowing her to revise and subvert a canonical narrative that would relegate the raced, gendered subject to silence and invisibility. Morrison not only challenges the kind of white-washing of Western culture and its traditions that would result in Bride's troubling erasure, she also constructs a vision of black female subjectivity that is compelling, and, at times, haunting, in order to draw the contemporary reader into the text. Beginning with Ovid as source material, Morrison weaves classical tales with a contemporary saga of black male-female relations, thereby re-inscribing the past through the lens of modernity. The author takes her novel to the figurative site of its literary predecessors in order to present a work that provides an alternate model of black, female identity.

Notes

1. Morrison, *God Help the Child* (Knopf, 2015), 8. Subsequent references to this edition are included parenthetically.

2. A number of reviewers offer commentary on Morrison's novel in terms of the author's indebtedness to the fairy tale. Among the more scathing early reviews is Tom Le Clair's "Toni Morrison Spins a Lame Fairy Tale" (*Daily Beast*, April 18, 2015). In a more balanced appraisal, Kara Walker describes the novel as "a brisk modern-day fairy tale with shades of the Brothers Grimm" ("Toni Morrison's 'God Help the Child,'" *New York Times*, April 13, 2015).

3. Morrison discusses the relationship between classical texts and black vernacular forms in Danielle Taylor-Guthrie, *Conversations with Toni Morrison* (UP of Mississippi, 1994), 101; 122; 176–77.

4. I am indebted to Edith Hamilton for insight into Greco-Roman mythology. See *Mythology: Timeless Tales of Gods and Heroes* (Little, Brown, 1942).

5. According to folklore and legend, butterflies function as a trope for reincarnation and transformation.

6. In the same way, the abusive Lenore doubles as the wicked stepmother in *Home*, a novelistic intervention into the classic fairy tale.

7. In *Home* the trip to Lotus, Georgia, on the part of Frank "Smart" Money assumes epic dimensions similar to Odysseus's journey to the underworld. Frank's evolving self-identity prompts a move from his perception of a world characterized by black-and-white to his realization of a range of colors, signified by Cee's quilt. *God Help the Child* lends itself to an ekphrastic analysis as well. Narrative emphasis on yellow directs attention to Morrison's reinscription of the trope of the animated statue as she creates a work of fiction that tries to relate to the realm of Greco-Roman art.

8. One is reminded of the Garners' nephews who steal Sethe's breast milk in *Beloved*. *Tar Baby*'s Mary Therese has breasts that produce milk continuously, as if to signify her embodiment of the "true and ancient properties" of maternity.

Works Cited

Bhabha, Homi. *The Location of Culture*. Routledge, 1994.

Brogan, Kathleen. *Cultural Haunting: Ghosts and Ethnicity in Recent American Literature*. UP of Virginia, 1998.

Butler, Judith. *Gender Trouble: Feminism and the Subversion of Identity*. Routledge, 1990.

Derrida, Jacques. "Structure, Sign and Play in the Discourse of the Human Sciences." *Writing and Difference*. Translated by Alan Bass. Routledge, 2001, 15–29.

Fanon, Frantz. *Black Skin, White Masks* [*Peau noire, masques blancs*, 1952]. Translated by Charles Lam Markmann. Grove Press, 1967.

Gabbin, Joanne. "A Laying on of Hands: Black Women Writers Exploring the Roots of Their Folk and Cultural Tradition." *Black Women in the Whirlwind: Afra-American Culture and the Contemporary Literary Renaissance*, edited by Joanne Braxton and A. N. McLaughlin. Rutgers UP, 1990, pp. 246–63.

Gilroy, Paul. *The Black Atlantic: Modernity and Double Consciousness*. Harvard UP, 1992.

Hamilton, Edith. *Mythology: Timeless Tales of Gods and Heroes*. Little, Brown, 1942.

Henderson, Mae Gwendolyn. "Speaking in Tongues: Dialogics, Dialectics, and the Black Woman Writer's Literary Tradition." *African-American Literary Theory: A Reader*, edited by Winston Napier. New York UP, 2000, 348–68.

Jones, Bessie W., and Audrey Vinson. "An Interview with Toni Morrison." *Conversations with Toni Morrison*, edited by Danielle Taylor-Guthrie. UP of Mississippi, 1994, pp. 171–87.

La Capra, Dominick. *Writing History, Writing Trauma*. Johns Hopkins UP, 2001.

Le Clair, Thomas. "The Language Must Not Sweat: A Conversation with Toni Morrison." *Conversations with Toni Morrison*, edited by Danielle Taylor-Guthrie UP of Mississippi, 1994, pp. 119–28.

Macksey, Richard, and Eugenio Donato, eds. *The Structuralist Controversy: The Languages of Criticism and the Sciences of Man*. Baltimore: Johns Hopkins UP, 1970.

Morrison, Toni. *God Help the Child*. Knopf, 2015.

———. *The Origin of Others*. Harvard UP, 2017.

———. *Playing in the Dark: Whiteness and the Literary Imagination*. Harvard UP, 1992.

———. "Rootedness: The Ancestor as Foundation." *Black Women Writers: A Critical Evaluation*, edited by Mari Evans. Anchor, 1984, pp. 339–45.

———. "Unspeakable Things Unspoken: The Afro-American Presence in American Literature." *Within the Circle: An Anthology of African-American Literary Criticism from the Harlem Renaissance to the Present*, edited by Angelyn Mitchell. Duke UP, 1994, pp. 368–98.

Roynon, Tessa. *Transforming American Culture: Toni Morrison and the Classical Tradition*. Oxford UP, 2013.

Ruas, Charles. "Toni Morrison." *Conversations with Toni Morrison*, edited by Danielle Taylor-Guthrie. UP of Mississippi, 1994, 93–118.

Schreiber, Evelyn Jaffe. *Race, Trauma, and Home in the Novels of Toni Morrison.* Louisiana State UP, 2010.

Valkeakari, Tuire. *Precarious Passages: The Diasporic Imagination in Contemporary Black Anglophone Fiction.* UP of Florida, 2017.

Wardi, Anissa J. *Water and African American Memory: An Eco-critical Perspective.* UP of Florida, 2011.

Section 3

Intertextual Interceptions

Return of the Repressed: The Politics of Engraving and Erasure and the Quest for Selfhood in *God Help the Child*

Justine Tally

Toni Morrison's eleven novels each deal with a specific historical period in the US (or the future US in the case of *A Mercy*) from the perspective of African Americans. Yet in an interview with Maddie Oatman for *Mother Jones*, she confesses that while working on her eleventh novel, "[I] was very nervous because I didn't have a handle on the contemporary. [. . .] It's very fluid." Despite this disclaimer Morrison very much locates *God Help the Child* (*GHTC*) within the concerns and sociopolitical situation in the US at the end of the twentieth century: pedophilia scandals within and without the Catholic Church, infectious diseases caught in the hospital, the criminally abusive system of prisons-for-profit that disproportionately targets blacks and other women/men of color ("Lucky for the state, crime does pay"[1]), the plastic nature of cosmetics and fashion as a literal cover-up for the lack of a true sense of self, the substitution of sexuality for love.[2] Perhaps less obvious but still crucial, the youth in the 1980s were called the "Me Generation," and the 1990s were denominated the "Age of Greed," in both cases intensifying a pervasive tendency to slough off responsibility for others and for one's actions. Elaine Showalter's book on *Hystories* (1997) is particularly relevant, specifically chapter 10 on "Recovered Memory," which includes narratives of "child abuse" guided by psychologists to incriminate innocent people and others by adults formulated in an attempt to duck responsibility for having done something personally considered morally reprehensible. From the beginning of the novel, Sweetness insists, "It's not my fault. So you can't blame me. I didn't do it and have no idea how it happened" (3), ostensibly referring to the very black skin of her daughter Lula Ann, as she and her husband are both "high yeller," almost white enough to pass. Unfortunately, by the end of the book she has learned nothing, still justifying her cruelty toward her daughter as a way to prepare her for life and exonerating herself from any responsibility. Taking responsibility for oneself and one's actions, however, entails a priori having a strong sense of self, something both Bride and Booker must search out in order to become whole.

While on first reading it becomes apparent that Bride in *God Help the Child* is Morrison's updated and reworked version of Pecola in *The Bluest Eye* (*TBE*), there are multiple intertextual references to her other novels as well: *Sula* turns up in Queen's fire, which, meant to cleanse the bedframe of bedbugs, turns lethal, a call to Eva's intentional setting fire to Plum to prevent him, in her vision, from crawling back into her womb or, more closely, to Hannah's being burned to death in spite of Eva's futile attempt to save her. *Sula* is also present in the rose tattoo that Booker wears on his shoulder in honor of his brother (which in turn calls to Tennessee Williams's play, a study in part of lies and deceit[3]). Booker's grandfather, Mr. Drew, like Milkman's father, Macon Dead, "[h]ad made his money as an unforgiving slumlord" (116). Booker "refused to think about the greed and criminality that produced his grandfather's fortune," money he inherits, which he justifies as "cleansed by death" (130). So much for intellectual purism.

Like Jadine in *Tar Baby*, Bride makes her career in fashion, which links her also to Hagar's obsession with cosmetics and the plastic world of consumerism. As in *Beloved* "ghosts" haunt Booker, not only his dead brother Adam, but also the "twin" that did not survive their birth (115). And the solace Booker finds in music echoes its importance in *Jazz*. The superficially perfect world of Ruby in *Paradise* with its direct call to *TBE* (perfect houses on perfect lawns which the Fathers are loath to have "contaminated," an imitation of the world of *Dick and Jane* which opens the first novel) contrasts surface with inner beauty, again clearly evident here in *GHTC*. Upon getting out of Decagon, Sofia is startled by "houses surrounded by grass so green it hurt my eyes. The flowers seem to be painted because I didn't remember roses that shade of lavender or sunflowers so blindingly bright" (68–69). In *Love* Morrison's rather visceral attack on the gratuitousness of sex as a substitution for "love" is echoed in Bride: before Booker, her "sex life became sort of like Diet Coke—deceptively sweet minus nutrition" (36).

Mediations and Inversions

Apart from the clearest calls to the importance of skin color and the rejection of the child by the mother, it would seem that too much of the negativity expressed in *The Bluest Eye* is still wreaking havoc on the characters in *God Help the Child*. Yet while images of popular culture continue to mediate reality, *GHTC* is set up more as an inverse reflection of *TBE*, important because it points to other aspects of the novel which are crucial for an in-depth understanding of its meaning. Pecola's yearning for blue eyes is echoed, on the one hand, in Bride's "alien eyes" so attractive to men, and on the other, in Julie's disabled daughter Molly (smothered by her mother, who is now an inmate at Decagon), who had "the loveliest blue eyes in the world" (67). Yet blackness as ugly in *The Bluest Eye* is replaced with blackness as "the hottest commodity in the civilized world" (36). Not only is "ideal" physical beauty perniciously flaunted in films and other cultural media (as seen in its pernicious influence on Pauline in *TBE*), but Bride also even learns "how to feel" from movies and magazine layouts, including what she never learns about Booker: "he confided nothing, so I just made stuff up with TV plots" (11). The importance of being loved in *TBE* ("how do you get somebody to love you?" [4]) is transported into the current novel through the yearning to be touched. Bride's first menstruation is met with fury by her mother, who first slaps her and then pushes her into a tub of cold water.[5] (Fortunately in *TBE*, Pecola's first menstruation, while initially shocking to her, is attended to first by Claudia and Frieda and then by the kindly Mrs. McTeer, who surrounds her with care, understanding, and song [*TBE* 31–32]).

Even so, Bride's shock was "alleviated by the satisfaction of being touched" (79). As a child Bride tries to incur her mother's anger so that Sweetness would hit her as punishment, perhaps, coupled with her sense of guilt, the psychological reason Bride so submissively accepts the physical pummeling by Sofia later. As a young adult she tries to recreate the sensuousness of sex with Booker, after he has left her, through tantalizing her skin with the long soft bristles on his shaving brush: "The silky hair is both tickly and soothing.... The satisfaction that follows is so so sweet" (34–35). But the sensual pleasure not only recalls the arousal Geraldine feels with her cat sitting on her loins in *TBE* (a substitute for sex with her husband) but also has a whiff of the film *Basic Instinct* (1992) in its contemporary fusion of sex with violence: "Brushing and then the razor, the combination that both excites and soothes me" (35).[6] Sensuality is relegated to vicarious pleasure, always more virtual than realized firsthand, and often a poor substitute for a real connection.

Booker's obsession with Bride is also a mediated affair. He himself is hardly immune to the influence of popular culture and media: "He and his dorm mates ranked girls according to men's magazines and porn videos, ranked one another according to characters in action movies they had seen" (121). He sees Bride as "a midnight Galatea" (132) and her blackness "thrilled him" (133). And yet

> six months into the bliss of edible sex,[7] free-style music, challenging books and the company of an easy undemanding Bride, the fairy-tale castle collapsed into the mud and sand on which its vanity was built. And Booker ran away. (135)

Their relationship, then, is also built on the mediation of literary and not-so-literary figures that they mistake for love, and as such it is built on shaky foundations and cannot withstand any stress.

Like the facade of Bride's beauty and her work in cosmetics, the work of this superficially accessible novel goes on sub rosa, another indication of both Bride's and Booker's hidden trauma. While the narrative of the novel seems deceptively simple, the description Bride gives early in the novel of her journey north is an indication of complications that should be signals to a careful reader: "I suppose other people might like the scenery bordering this highway but it's so thick with lanes, exits, parallel roads, overpasses, cautionary signals and signs it's like being forced to read a newspaper while driving. Annoying" (13). The "re-write" of Pecola's story of descent into madness certainly provides another cautionary tale. Bride is hugely successful but still relying on "skin" for her sense of identity, as Jeri, her stylist, insists that "Black sells. It's the hottest commodity in the civilized world" (36), the inverse lesson driven relentlessly home by her mother. Convinced as a child, like Pecola, that blackness is ugly, Bride/Lula Ann interiorizes what Morrison has referred to as one of the most pernicious ideas of the Western world—external appearance and white norms of physical attractiveness: "[H]ow well beauty worked. She had not known its shallowness or her own cowardice—the vital lesson Sweetness taught and nailed to her spine to curve it" (151). For all her commercial success, Bride's psyche is engraved with feelings of inferiority. How she comes to erase those feelings is the project of the novel.

Engraving and Erasure

Two issues of significant import in this novel are those of *engraving* and *erasure*, a study of what a "memorial" to loss should look like, and the relationship of both to the formation of a sense of self. And in this sense *God Help the Child* is most seriously involved in questioning the hard work laid out in *Beloved*: the role of memory in life as lived and in the development of an adult personality.

Recovering from a ferocious beating from her confrontation with Sofia, Bride rails against boredom, finding that "memory is the worst thing about healing" (29). Yet even convalescing back at home she is out-of-sorts, impatient with "fake" friends, "who come here just to gaze and pity me. I can't watch television; it's so boring—mostly blood, lipstick, and the haunches of anchorgirls. What passes for news is either gossip or a lecture of lies" (29). Even the weather channels, which she describes as "the only informative sources, [. . .] were off-base and hysterical most of the time" (112). Contemporary actresses are cookie-cutter in nature: [I]n the forties or fifties [...] film stars had distinguishing faces unlike now, when hairstyles alone separated one star from another" (86). Such conformity means that contemporary actresses and televisions news anchors are basically indistinguishable and are therefore easily "erased," as they have no distinguishing features or personality.

Moreover, Booker's last name, Starbern, evokes ephemerality: "[S]tars can explode, disappear. Besides, what we see when we look at them may no longer be there" (163).[8] Yet later, in one of his letters, Booker recognizes that his devotion to his murdered brother has also resulted in a kind of erasure: "I miss the emotion that your dying produced a feeling so strong it defined me while it erased you leaving only your absence for me to live in" (161). There are smaller incidences of erasure found in the traces of the former inhabitants of the California forests; Bride drives down "dirt roads as old as the Tribes" (80), roads "created originally by moccasin-shod feet and wolf packs" (141); the forests themselves are then erased by loggers (168). Even the "very old, rumpled doctor," Walter Muskie, who jokes about the profusion of letters after his name, indicative of titles, including "DDT" (88), conjures up times gone by: Walt (Whitman), "democratic" poet of the nineteenth century, celebrator of a country of workers and early Natives and settlers now erased by time, in perfect harmony with the "aging hippies" who have taken Bride in to convalesce.

Although Booker attempts to memorialize his gesture at Adam's funeral by tattooing (engraving) a rose on his left shoulder (120), his proposal to his family for a memorial to their eldest son falls flat: "When he visited his and Adam's old bedroom, the thread of disapproval he'd felt during his proposal of a memorial became a rope, as he saw the savage absence not only of Adam but of himself" (125). The physical disappearance of Adam from the family home is also Booker's own erasure. Yet, interestingly, it is easier for Booker to see Bride's subjugation to engraving and erasure than his own. In his letter he writes, "You accepted like a beast of burden the whip of a stranger's curse and the mindless menace it holds along with the scar it leaves as a definition you spend your life refuting although that hateful word is only a slim line drawn on a shore and quickly dissolved in a seaworld" (149). Only at the end of the novel does Booker understand how badly their relationship has been distorted by a lack of communication, the suppression of their fears and feelings of inferiority to the point of erasure of any meaningful sharing. To Queen's query as to "what caused the split" between Booker and Bride, he answers, "Lies. Silence. Just not saying what was true or why" (155).

The significance of "erasure" is most obviously referenced in the description of what happens to Bride herself as she imagines herself regressing into a child's body: first, the feeling of "melting away" (8), then the closing of the tiny holes in her earlobes (50), and the disappearance of her tastebuds (30), later emphasized by the flattening of her breasts, lack of pubic hair, and hairless underarms (97). The adult Bride devolves into the child Lula Ann, representing the collapse of her fragile sense of self. Her most serious problem when Booker walks out is precisely that she feels "Dismissed. Erased" (38), a feeling repeated in her confrontation turned violent with Sofia ("Even Sofia Huxley, of all people, erased me.... I'm not sure which is worse, being dumped like trash or whipped like a slave" [38]).

However, the question of how and how much to remember is a prickly one. Queen's gallery of photographs of her daughter Hannah looks to Booker more like a "memorial." Adam's murderer/molester ("the nicest man in the world") had engraved the names of his victims across his shoulders (118) and kept photographs of each little boy in his den (169) ... not to mention preserving their penises in a decorated candy box (119), a "memorial" to his own perversion. Even Adam's own memorial tattoo loses its shape and becomes unrecognizable to Bride as anything other than an amorphous orange blob. When is memory so overpowering that it conditions the present? How do we remember without memorializing? When is it time to let go of the trauma? And how do we do so? At the end of the novel, Booker "erases" the physical evidence of what had been most meaningful in his life—Queen's ashes and his beloved trumpet, "one by fire, one by water, two of what he had so intensely loved gone!" (174)—an act that frees him from the past in order to contemplate a future with Bride and their unborn child. Yet even Sofia finds Bride's pearl earring and keeps it in her wallet, "as what? A kind of remembrance?" (77)

A traumatic childhood may inform the future, but it must not be allowed to determine it; it is necessary to try to let devastating memories go. *God Help the Child* is full of child abuse on many levels, but "only by forging meaningful relationships can the individual transcend the agony of alienated existence and achieve wholeness" (Munro 154). Even Sweetness, given the last section in the book, expresses some regret but ultimately refuses to dwell on it and take any responsibility: "No. I have to push those memories away—fast. No point. I know I did the best for her under the circumstances." (177). Erasure cuts both ways. "Memory makes life pleasant, forgetfulness makes it possible," as even Queen is "grateful that, at last, Sweet Jesus had given her a forgetfulness blanket along with a little pillow of wisdom to comfort her in old age" (159).

Bride's physical "erasure" in the novel, however, is much more meaningful than a simple return to her childish state or a rewrite of Pecola's plight in *The Bluest Eye*.[9] Bride starts her search for Booker to find out what he meant by "You not the woman I want." Even she has noted her own lack of self in inadvertently replying "neither am I" (10). These protagonists' individual quests are not actually for each other but for selfhood, sine qua non for being able to love another. As Bride progressively "loses" the physical attributes that would make her a woman, and is taken in by Steve and Evelyn, two "aging hippies," she meets a version of her child-self in Rain, whose street smarts have helped her survive, as she was also neglected and mistreated by her mother. Rain is at once exceedingly curious about Bride and becomes much attached to her because Bride listens to what she has to say. Rain is also particularly fond of the hookers on the corner who provide her with useful information for survival, much as Pecola, her mother absent, recurs to the friendship of the three whores in *TBE*. Understanding Rain's metaphorical function in the novel opens an additional window on Bride's quest for selfhood.

Projection of the Self: Bride and Rain

The appearance of Rain is more than coincidental; she is crucial to the story and has been announced surreptitiously from the beginning, setting both the plot and the themes of the novel in motion. When Booker's idea for a memorial for Adam is rejected by his family, "[i]t was fitting, perhaps . . . he would step out into a downpour. Rain forced him to raise his collar and duck his head like an intruder thankful for the night. Shoulders high, eyes squinting, he moved down Decatur Street in a mood the rainstorm complemented (124)." This rejection sets the course for his gig playing trumpet in a band, and then with other musicians on the street, and his (eventual) spotting of Bride for the first time. Booker, "dumbstruck" by Bride's unusual beauty, decides to play his trumpet as usual, but it is "only then that he notices the rain—soft, steady." "He decided to play his trumpet alone in the rain anyway"; "Low, muted notes held long, too long, as the strains floated through drops of rain"; "the rain-soaked air smelled like lilac when he played while remembering her" (131). Rain is mentioned four times on one page as Booker remembers seeing Bride.

Appropriately, the day after Booker walks out on Bride, it begins to rain: "Bullet taps on the windows followed by crystal lines of water" (9). Her attempts to beat back any "tiny ripple of missing him" sets her on her quest first to see Sofia as she leaves prison, so as to offer material recompense for the harm Bride had caused her, and later to find Booker. On her way to the town of Whiskey to find Booker, Bride misses a tight turn in the road and spins the Jaguar off into a tree, described as the Tree of Origin ("what must have been the world's first and biggest tree" [82]), reinforcing the return to beginnings evident in the slow erasure of her physical self. Trapped and close to hysteria, she is finally found by a "girl, very young, carrying a black kitten, [. . .] with the greenest eyes Bride had ever seen" (83).[10] Later, Evelyn introduces her more formally: "Bride, this is Raisin. Actually we named her Rain because that is where we found her, but she prefers to call herself Raisin" (86).

Thereafter, almost every time Rain appears, the narrator remarks on her physical appearance, with particular reference to her eyes: green-eyed girl (84), emerald-eyed girl (85), emerald-eyed girl (86), milk-white skin, ebony hair, neon eyes, undetermined age (86). Rain describes her street smarts to Bride, "her emerald eyes sometimes sparkling wide other times narrowed to dark olive slits" (102). It is noteworthy that aside from her deep dark blackness, Bride's most outstanding feature is also her eyes. Brooklyn remarks, "Alien eyes, I call them, but guys think they're gorgeous, of course" (23); for Jeri they are "wolverine eyes"; Sofia does not recognize her at first, but "something about her eyes seemed familiar" (69). Bride's blackness "thrilled" Booker, but he consistently raves about her eyes: "he watched her mesmerizing eyes . . . speaking-eyes . . . as well as those eyes [. . .] more exquisite, more aesthetically pleasing because of her obsidian-midnight skin; [. . .] he could always see starlight in her eyes" (133). Even Rain notes that "her black lady" has eyes that scared her at first but are like those of her cat, Silky (104), that is, green like Rain's. It is noteworthy that because Morrison does not usually dwell on the physical features of her characters, her emphasis on the physical characteristics of both Rain and Bride sharpens their connection: Rain is set up as a projection of Bride's erased childhood and sense of self. As Bride loses the attributes she associates with her womanhood, losing weight dramatically, Evelyn exchanges her jeans "for a pair of Rain's, which fit Bride perfectly" (93).

Bride's unusual empathy for Rain surprises her. Listening to Rain's story, "Bride fought against the danger of tears for anyone other than herself. . . . [S]he felt a companionship that was surprisingly free of envy. Like the closeness of schoolgirls" (103). When Evelyn tells Bride how they found the child in the rain, Bride shuddered, "as though it were she herself in that alley" (96). And when Bride wakes up in the middle of the night to find Rain standing over her and tries to speak to her, "she seemed to disappear" (97). Bride is "haunted" by her own ghostly child-self. The stark difference in their skin colors sets up a "positive-negative" picture in which Rain is the exact inverse reflection of Bride. Although Jean Wyatt argues that Bride learns to be the mother she never had through caring for Rain, I would argue rather that this is a metaphorical relationship in which Bride learns to take responsibility and care for herself. As a baby/child who was never nurtured or even touched, Bride would have been classified as a "frozen baby"[11] whose prognosis would be to grow up unfeeling and unable to relate at all to others. Rather than a more realistic approach, this novel is more usefully read as an allegory. While I do agree with Wyatt when she writes that "the narration of *God Help the Child* betrays an impatience with the residues of trauma that hold back its characters from loving anew" (171), the overriding question that Morrison deals with is how to move beyond being ensnared and stifled by the trauma. Childhood trauma may come from within or without the family,[12] leading to an erasure of the "self" and its substitution by superficial features, that is, Bride's obsession with her commodified beauty and her subsequent narcissism: "Her self-love was consistent with her cosmetic company milieu and mirrored his obsession with her" (133). Booker's psychological growth has been stunted as well by his obsession with Adam and his refusal to let the past go.

The Quest for Selfhood

Wyatt argues that *GHTC* is a romance and that "[t]he quest that determines the sequence of her narrated chapters is [...] straightforward: abandoned by Booker, Bride sets out to find him, and in the end succeeds" (172). But this idea is belied by the narration:

> The reason for this tracking was *not love*, she knew; it was more hurt than anger that made her drive into unknown territory to locate the one person she once trusted, who made her feel safe, colonized somehow (78; emphasis added).[13]

Later, in Whiskey, talking things through with Queen, Bride eventually reaches a conclusion: "Damn!" Bride slapped the table. "You're absolutely right! Totally right! *This is about me*, not him. *Me*!" (152; emphasis added). The realization leads her to a brawl with Booker and her ultimate confession of having lied in court to convict Sofia in order to finally earn the approval of her mother and other adults.

Interpreting the novel as a romantic quest creates more problems than it solves. Wyatt herself questions the disparate nature of the two protagonists, "so seemingly incompatible" (173), and finds their newfound relationship to be based on the resolution of the "conflict between past trauma and present love" (180). Yet though Wyatt is willing to accept the intercession of Queen "to interpret the bodily form that Booker's grieving takes, the devolution of Bride's body remains unexplained" (180). She surmises that "Bride's transformation into the body of a little black girl [is] a corporeal representation of her temptation to remain the child victim of trauma" (184). Except that it may not be actually "corporeal" at all, in that Bride is the only one who notices the changes in her body, with the possible exception of the fact that she fits into Rain's jeans. But even there we are not privy to actual sizes before and after, just that Rain is a little girl of undetermined age and Evelyn is "a tall woman with unfashionable hips" (86); Bride, on the other hand, is complacent knowing that she doesn't "need silicon in [her] butt" (57), which indicates that Evelyn's jeans would never have fit her in the first place. Indeed, Morrison herself states that Bride is "very successful—you know, the 'panther in snow.' But *in her brain*, she's returning to that despised little black girl her mother didn't even like" (Oatman; emphasis added). This idea is reinforced in the third-person section but focalized through Bride's point of view: "Flat-chested and without underarm or pubic hair, pierced ears and stable weight, she tried and failed to forget *what she believed* was her crazed transformation back into a scared little black girl" (142; emphasis added).

The Bride/Rain dichotomy might therefore be interpreted as a projection of Bride's own childhood frustration, longing, and anger, also exemplified in Sofía's "gratitude" to Bride for having given her both the tears to cry away the pain[14] and the opportunity to fight back against her own "mother." That Sofia has also experienced a return to childhood is clear in her reaction to her release from Decagon: "I felt like a little kid seeing the world for the first time" (68). In return for Bride's offer of money and cosmetics, Sofia beats Bride black and blue, as

> kicking and punching her freed me up more than being paroled. I felt I was ripping blue-and-white wallpaper, returning slaps and running the devil Mommy knew so well out of my life.
> [...]
> When I tend to my patients [...] in my mind I am putting the black girl back together, healing her, thanking her. For the release.
> Sorry Mommy. (77)

In Freudian terms, Sofia displaces her childhood rage against her own mother, using "an unconscious defense mechanism whereby the mind substitutes either a new aim or a new object for goals felt in their original form to be dangerous or unacceptable," which is certainly the case in that Sofia has repressed the resentment of her mother: "The aggressive drive—mortido—may be displaced quite as much as the libidinal. In such scapegoating, aggression may be displaced onto people with little or no connection with what is causing anger" ("Displacement").[15] This aggressive reaction is also manifest in Booker, twice in the novel,[16] to compensate for his feelings of impotence and rage over the sexual torture and murder of his brother, and is also behind his abandonment of Bride on discovering that she wants to help a presumed child molester. Another form of displacement is found in Queen's children sending her money—"Most of them send me money so they don't have to come see me" (146–47)—which is an exact mirror of Bride's attitude toward her own mother. Scrappy Brooklyn cannot help but eye Bride's position at Sylvia, Inc. (26), even as she helps her "friend" through the necessary medical examinations and then on home. Though a relatively minor yet supportive character in the novel, Brooklyn also left home at an early age (only fourteen), running away from an alcoholic mother and having to "reinvent" and "toughen" herself (140). As the child of an alcoholic mother, she has also been deprived of a "normal" childhood and manifests certain characteristics common to children of alcoholics, including mistrust, an acute need for control, leading to manipulation, and an extreme sense of loyalty even when faced with someone who does not "deserve" it.[17]

Rather than a romantic quest, I would argue that both Bride and Booker are on a quest for their "selves," heretofore stunted by the traumatic experiences of their childhood, experiences that have turned the focus of these two protagonists into a "narcissistic preoccupation with the self" (Lasch 150). Lynn Munro recurs to Lasch's argument for its special bearing on Williams's *The Rose Tattoo* and Morrison's *Sula* insofar as a narcissistic culture "has translated the predatory individualism of the American Adam into a therapeutic jargon that celebrates not so much the individualism as solipsism, justifying absorption as 'authenticity' and 'awareness'" (370); Booker's rose tattoo in memory of his murdered brother Adam also calls intertextually to these earlier works. Munro alleges that Serafina and Sula have both "deceived themselves. They have asserted what resembles a solipsistic obsession with inner truths, and they have both, as a result, become crippled and alienated" (153), which certainly describes Booker as well. Bride also echoes Sula's plight: [A]t the conclusion of the relationship [Sula] is left questioning whether, in fact, she ever knew anything about [Ajax]" (153).

> Queen: "You sound like you don't know him too good."
> Bride: "I don't, but I thought I did." She didn't say so but it suddenly occurred to her that good sex was not knowledge. It was barely information. (146)

The denouement of the novel is centered on this quest for knowledge of the self and of others. Reminiscent of the burning of Plum (intentionally) and of Hannah (accidentally), Queen's accidental fire, from which Booker and Bride heroically pull her,[18] lands her in the hospital with serious burns while Bride and Booker wait on her hand and foot. Booker's insistence on washing Queen's feet himself is indicative of his newfound (Christlike) humility in caring for someone besides himself. "They worked together like a true couple, thinking not of themselves, but of helping somebody else" (167), an idea repeated only five pages later: "These last days [. . .] were congenial because their focus was on a third person they both loved" (172). This devotion to Queen begins to erase their own solipsistic narcissism, finally liberating them through the selfless love of and care for another person. For the first time in their lives, their attention is focused totally outside of themselves, allowing them to renew their own relationship through their newfound sense of identity.[19] Herein lies the meaning of Morrison's words in her *Mother Jones* interview with Oatman: "[Bride's] beauty is beyond makeup—and so she feels perfect. That's not enough for me. You have to be a complete human being, and that has to do with your generosity. That's what I wanted for her to encounter." And ultimately that is what is cohesive about the ending of the novel. In spite of Sweetness's skepticism, their impending parenthood[20] will (hopefully) imply this generosity of spirit toward each other and toward this new addition to their world.

Paradoxically, it seems, a sense of self is found only in selflessness.

Notes

1. Toni Morrison, *God Help the Child* (London: Chatto & Windus, 2015), p. 13. All other citations to this novel will refer to this edition and will be included in the text proper. Just as Pecola's surname, Breedlove, is the maiden name of Madame C. J. Walker (Sarah Breedlove), the woman who built a fortune selling beauty products to African American women, credited with being the first self-made female African American millionaire, and a generous philanthropist, Lula Ann's last name (originally) is Bridewell, which refers to "a house of correction; jail, especially for minor offences (originally St. Bride's Well), a house of correction in London in the sixteenth century. Online at http://www.thefreedictionary.com/Bridewell; accessed July 24th, 2017. "From 1980 to 2014, the rate of growth in the number of women in prison outpaced that of men by more than 50 percent (and black women continue to be incarcerated at twice the rate of white women)." See Andrea J. Ritchie, "A Warrant to Search Your Vagina," *New York Times* (July 21, 2017). Online at https://www.nytimes.com/2017/07/21/opinion/sunday/black-women-police-brutality.html. Accessed July 27, 2017. Sofia's remark on seeing Bride is pertinent: "In another world her black skin would have been remarkable, but living all those years in Decagon it wasn't" (69).

2. "[Bride's] self-love was consistent with her cosmetics company milieu and mirrored [Booker's] obsession with her" (133).

3. That Queen dies in her bed is another perhaps more subtle reference to *The Rose Tattoo*. Serafina commemorates her passion for Rosario thusly: "To me the big bed was beautiful like a religion. Now I lie on it with dreams, with memories only! But it is still beautiful to me" (Williams 196–97).

4. Toni Morrison, *The Bluest Eye* (New York: Penguin, 1993) p. 32.

5. Cf. Pauline in *TBE* who comforts the white child rather than Pecola, whose skin has been burned by the cobbler, and who is also ferociously slapped by her mother (*TBE*, p.109.)

6. The text does not make clear whether Bride is actually shaving herself.

7. A call to Connie in *Paradise*.

8. I believe that Wyatt misreads this image when she alleges that "one must continue steadfast through the burning-up for as long as heart-break lasts—which, the image of the star suggests, might be as long as forever" (175). On page 163 of the novel, Morrison writes,

> Bride: "You still believe heartbreak should burn like a star?"
> Booker [Starbern]: "But stars can explode, disappear. Besides, what we see when we look at them may no longer be there." (163)

9. In anguish over all the ugliness she perceives in her life, Pecola tries to make herself disappear bit by bit, though she never manages to erase her eyes. (*TBE* 45).

10. Note another inversion in that Geraldine's totally black cat has startling blue eyes.

11. "Reactive attachment disorder can result when children do not form normal healthy relationships and *attachments* with adult caregivers during the first few years of childhood. Symptoms of the disorder include being withdrawn from adult caregivers and social and emotional disturbances that result from patterns of insufficient care and neglect" (Cherry "List"). "While attachment styles displayed in adulthood are not necessarily the same as those seen in infancy, research indicates that early attachments can have a serious impact on later relationships. (Cherry "Bowlby").

12. Certainly Booker's mother and father have created a loving stable environment up to Adam's abduction, abuse, and murder, countering Wyatt's assertion that all the mothers in the novel are "terrible" (176). For a more in-depth discussion of motherhood, see also Tiwari.

13. "Colonized," and therefore with no sense of real self.

14. "The release of tears unshed for fifteen years.... Now I am clean and able" (70).

15. "My parents [...] never wrote, called or visited. I wasn't surprised. They were always hard to please. The family Bible was placed on a stand right next to the piano, where my mother played hymns after supper. They never said so, but I suspect they were glad to be rid of me. In their world of God and Devil no innocent person is sentenced to prison" (68)

16. Once against the exhibitionist in the park, and again against the parents so drugged they are ignoring their very young child.

17. See, for example, Clancey, Martin, and Uscher.

18. And it's relevant to note that when Bride pulls off her own shirt to wrap Queen's head to smother the fire, she is surprised (and delighted in spite of the turmoil) to find that her breasts have "returned" to being "lovely" and "plump" (166).

19. Booker is surprised but pleased that Bride has "changed from one dimension into three—demanding, perceptive, daring" 173), and at last he opens his own eyes to the realization that his need to believe that he was a talented trumpet player hid his own limitations.

20. Bride's pregnancy is foreshadowed by her "strangely delayed menstrual period" (95), reaffirmed on page 142: "Although there were no more physical disappearances, she was disturbed by the fact that she'd had no menstrual period for at least two, maybe three, months." Therefore, the changes she "perceives" in her body are subject to both psychological and physical causes.

Works Cited

Cherry, Kendra "A List of Psychological Disorders." https://www.verywell.com/a-list-of-psychological-disorders-2794776 . Accessed July 27, 2017.

———. "Bowlby & Ainsworth: What Is Attachment Theory? The Importance of Early Emotional Bonds." https://www.verywell.com/what-is-attachment-2794822. Accessed October 17, 2019.

Clancey, Dawn. "5 Characteristics of Adult Children of Alcoholics." https://www.thefix.com/content/5-characteristics-adult-children-alcoholics. Accessed on August 3, 2017.

"Displacement (Psychology)." https://en.wikipedia.org/wiki/Displacement_%28psychology%29. Accessed August 30, 2017.

Lasch, Christopher. "Afterword: The Culture of Narcissism Revisited," in *The Culture of Narcissism: American Life in an Age of Diminishing Expectations*. W. W. Norton, 1979. New ed. 1991.

Martin, Sharon, LCSW. "Adult Children of Alcoholics and the Need to Feel in Control." https://blogs.psychcentral.com/imperfect/2017/04/adult-children-of-alcoholics-and-the-need-to-feel-in-control/. Accessed on March 3, 2017.

Morrison, Toni. *The Bluest Eye*. Penguin, 1993.

———. *God Help the Child*. Chatto & Windus, 2015.

Munro, Lynn. "The Tattooed Heart and the Serpentine Eye: Morrison's Choice of an Epigraph for *Sula*." *Black American Literature Forum*, Vol. 18, no. 4,1984, pp. 150–54. http://www.jstor.org/stable/2904290. Access 08-May-2017.

Oatman, Maddie. "Toni Morrison Knows All about the 'Little Drop of Poison' in Your Childhood." *Mother Jones*, April 21, 2015. http://www.motherjones.com/media/2015/04/toni-morrison-interview-god-help-the-child/. Access 24-Julyl-2017.

Showalter, Elaine. *Hystories: Hysterical Epidemics and Modern Media*. Columbia University Press, 1997.

Stepto, Robert B. "'Intimate Things in Place': A Conversation with Toni Morrison," *Massachusetts Review*, vol. 18, no. 3 1977, pp. 473–89.

Tiwari, Kusha. "Unmothered Children and Disruptive Innocence in Toni Morrison's *God Help the Child*." *Toni Morrison: Critical Perspectives*, edited by Kusha Tiwari. Pencraft International, 2017, pp. 236–47.

Uscher, Jen. "Adult Children of Alcoholics." http://www.webmd.com/mental-health/addiction/features/adult-children-of-alcoholics#1. Accessed on August, 3, 2017.

Wyatt, Jean. "Love, Trauma, and the Body in *God Help the Child*." *Love and Narrative Form in Toni Morrison's Later Novels*. U of Georgia P, 2017, pp. 171–87.

Williams, Tennessee. *The Rose Tattoo. Three by Tennessee*. New American Library, 1976, pp. 123–253.

No System of Justice: At the Margins with Toni Morrison's Intertextual Characters

Alice Knox Eaton

I began reading Toni Morrison by accident when I was thirteen. I was in the habit of reading my older sister's books, and she had checked *The Bluest Eye* out of the library. I admired the beautiful woman with the beautiful Afro on the back cover, and I got lost in the language of the story. I knew that someday I would understand it better, but what I did understand helped me a great deal. Claudia, Frieda, Maureen Peal, and, of course, Pecola, gave me a story that made sense out of what I was seeing at my junior high school.

I watched black girls mock other black girls about their different shades of skin color. One girl was too light and perceived as a snob; very dark girls were called ugly. I was white, blonde, blue-eyed; my skin color gave me a pass, and I was merely mocked for my bookishness. Still, I felt for Pecola and thanked Morrison silently for giving me an emerging understanding of colorism, a context for the charged hallways of my school.

I didn't read Morrison again until after college, ten years later, in 1981. Out of school for the first time since I was a child, giddy at the pleasure of choosing my own reading, I found a review of *Tar Baby* splashed across the *New York Times Book Review*. I remembered the wise woman who had helped me navigate junior high, and I gasped at the beautiful and raw sexuality of Jadine and Son. I read *Song of Solomon* and *Sula*, and reread *The Bluest Eye* in quick succession. Like so many readers, I felt Morrison was speaking directly to me, and I waited impatiently for her next book. I reserved a copy of *Beloved* in advance at the Brooklyn Public Library; I was the first reader of that particular copy in 1987.

I did not become a scholar of Morrison until I began graduate school in 1991, twenty years after I had first encountered her. Even now, when I read a new Morrison novel, I am a reader first, a scholar later. I measure the new book against the ones that came before, with my own personal compass. Eventually, I layer in other readers' and scholars' takes on the novels, but with each new book I tap into the wonder I felt at thirteen reading *The Bluest Eye*. With the publication of *God Help the Child* in 2015, due to its distinct resonance with *The Bluest Eye*, my response to the novel ran the full arc of my nearly fifty years of reading Morrison's works, drawing on personal and scholarly engagement with her characters simultaneously, producing an inevitably intertextual response to her last novel.

Intertextual Interceptions

Morrison has written of seeing herself as a reader as much as a writer; her now-famous instruction "If there's a book that you want to read, but it hasn't been written yet, then you must write it" speaks to her initial impulse for writing her first novel, *The Bluest Eye*, from the perspective of a reader. In discussing intertextuality, Julia Kristeva writes:

> The writer's interlocutor [. . .] is the writer himself, but as reader of another text. The one who writes is the same as the one who reads. Since his interlocutor is a text, he himself is no more than a text rereading itself. (quoted in Martínez Alfaro 277).

Morrison can be seen as rereading and rewriting her own texts in a stream of intertextual interplay. Indeed, all prolific writers can be read this way, from William Shakespeare to William Faulkner to Jodi Picoult. Like any writer, Morrison revisits and reimagines certain predominant themes throughout her eleven novels, one short story, and numerous works of nonfiction.

In her essay "Contextualizing Toni Morrison's Ninth Novel: What Mercy? Why Now?," Justine Tally catalogs a wide range of intertextual references in Morrison's novels up through *A Mercy*. Tally convincingly links Morrison's oeuvre to texts by Phillis Wheatley, Harriet Jacobs, W.E.B. Du Bois, Nathaniel Hawthorne, and F. Scott Fitzgerald. My focus in the intertextuality of Morrison's output is more narrow: I am interested in how her own works interact with each other, and where the fictional worlds of each of her individual novels overlap, even merge into a single identifiable Morrisonian universe, from *The Bluest Eye* in 1970 to *God Help the Child* in 2015.

Morrison's most striking intertextual characters occur in two of her most celebrated novels, *Beloved* and *Jazz*. The last we see of the title character of *Beloved*, she is naked and hugely pregnant. Then she disappears, with a whisper of trees in the woods, as if she has been whisked back into their leafy embrace. As a ghost, Beloved the character has the capability of appearing and disappearing at will, and her intense haunting at the end of the novel has reached its culmination, so the embodied version of Beloved reverts back to rustles in the trees, fleeting glances out of family photographs, and finally, simply "weather."

In the middle of Morrison's next novel, *Jazz*, an identical naked, hugely pregnant black woman with long roped hair bursts into the narrative. When asked by an interviewer if this new character was Beloved in a new form, Morrison conceded that it was possible but did not elaborate.[1] Beloved's disappearance into the woods, and this new character's bursting out of a different set of woods in *Jazz*, functions as a portal between the two novels.

The transient nature of the two characters is reinforced by their naming. Both sport adjectival names, Wild and Beloved, and their presence in the novels serves as a description of a state of mind for the characters around them. Their presence as characters in their own right is elusive and always contingent on the actions of others.

Martha Cutter illuminates the larger purpose of Morrison's intertextual strategy between the two novels:

> the intertextuality between *Jazz* and *Beloved* [creates] a story that resists closure through its very awareness of the reader's need for closure, and its simultaneous insistence that closure itself is a delusion, an impulse that must at all times and in all ways be deconstructed and undermined.

[...] To keep stories alive and in memory, they must be told and retold—
the story must go on and on to survive. (62)

Pecola Breedlove's story in Morrison's first novel is told and retold in her eleventh novel through the main character, Lula Ann Bridewell, called Bride.

God Help the Child reminded me that I had always felt a lingering worry about Pecola. What happened to her, after the story ended with her stepping like a wounded bird amid the trash of Lorain, Ohio? Where had this imagined character gone to in the Morrison canon? Encountering Morrison's new character Bride in *God Help the Child*, I felt a zing of recognition. Emotionally, Bride inhabits the same landscape as Pecola. Bride is Pecola resurrected. Reading *God Help the Child*, I had to continually remind myself that the story takes place in the early twenty-first century, in the decade of its publication, not in the 1930s Lorain, Ohio, of *The Bluest Eye*. Bride's first-person narration carries a burden of wisdom that seems too heavy for her twenty-three years. Ultimately, the era in which *God Help the Child* is set is less important than the timeless themes of the novel, echoing and building on Morrison's previous novels: trauma and recovery, mothers and children, the wounds of internalized racism and intra-community colorism. Pecola, the black girl who longs for blue eyes, dormant for the stretch of ten novels and forty-five years of Morrison's storied career, crosses from the author's first novel into her eleventh in the character of Bride.

Born Lula Ann Bridewell, Bride is blue-black and strikingly beautiful as a grown woman, advised by a stylist to always wear white to play up her deep blackness, to make it an asset, not a deficit, in the world of superficial physical beauty. It was not always so. Bride's own mother, Sweetness, was horrified at her daughter's dark skin; Sweetness herself was a "high yellow" woman with deeply entrenched color snobbery. Her husband, too, was light-skinned, and he could never believe that Sweetness did not cheat on him with a darker man, though Sweetness asserts her husband's paternity throughout the novel.

Nearly identical scenes of postpartum mother and child provide a portal between the two novels. In *The Bluest Eye*, Pecola is also blue-black. Her mother, Pauline, had a visceral, negative response to her dark-skinned child just after she was born: "She looked different from what I thought.... A right smart baby she was.... But I knowed she was ugly. Head full of pretty hair, but Lord she was ugly" (125–26).

Sweetness's response to baby Lula Ann provides a remarkable parallel to Pauline's response to Pecola. Both mothers reject their daughters in similar post-birth scenes. Here is Sweetness:

> I hate to say it, but from the very beginning in the maternity ward the baby, Lula Ann, embarrassed me. Her birth skin was pale like all babies', even African ones, but it changed fast. I thought I was going crazy when she turned blue-black before my eyes. I know I went crazy for a minute because once—just for a few seconds—I held a blanket over her face and pressed. But I couldn't do that, no matter how much I wished she hadn't been born with that terrible color. (4–5)

In *The Bluest Eye*, Morrison describes the Breedlove family as possessing an ugliness that was "unique. No one could have convinced them that they were not relentlessly ugly" (38). She writes further that the Breedloves "wore their ugliness, put it on, so to speak, although it did not belong to them.... You looked at them and wondered why they were so ugly; you looked closely and could not find the source. Then you realized that it came from conviction, their conviction" (39).

Both Pecola and Lula Ann are born into a state of being distasteful to look at, deemed so by their own mothers. In Sweetness's case, her daughter's blackness is an affront to her own carefully cultivated "high yellow" skin, preserved through the colorism of black social clubs reserved for the light-skinned, because, she asserts, "how else can we maintain a little dignity?" (4). Pecola's ugliness is passed on to her through her own mother's conviction that she herself is ugly.[2]

By the end of *The Bluest Eye*, Pecola is destroyed: slapped and dismissed by her mother in favor of the little white girl she works for, raped and impregnated by her father. Her tragedy becomes a source of delicious gossip. Though her father is imprisoned for the rape, Morrison makes it clear that there is no system of justice that can save Pecola from the racism of the wider world, even, or especially, within her own community. Pecola's friends Claudia and Frieda listen in horror as the black women in their neighborhood say that Pecola "carry some of the blame" for her rape and subsequent pregnancy (189). To her young friends' further astonishment, the women say of Pecola's baby: "She be lucky if it don't live. Bound to be the ugliest thing walking" (189).

Pecola is destroyed, not just by a lack of mother-love and the brutality of her father, but by an internalized self-hatred in the wider black community that buys into white standards of beauty. Her parents are victims of the same self-hatred, and Pecola is its most vulnerable casualty, disappearing into an impenetrable madness after her baby does indeed die. Her madness allows her to achieve her impossible wish for blue eyes, the one thing that comforts her in her bleak, stunted life.

(No) Systems of Justice

God Help the Child contains the only courtroom scene in all of Toni Morrison's novels, where readers witness a miscarriage of justice. The scene is narrated from a distance of years, through Bride's first-person narration of when she served as a witness in a child abuse case, and lasts less than a page. Morrison has no interest in dramatizing the workings of the so-called justice system. Her novels are filled with villains and victims, but redemption, if it comes at all, comes through means outside the law. In *The Bluest Eye*, the father-rapist of the main character does end up in jail, but that fact is noted peremptorily at the end of the novel; Morrison's focus is on the damage done to the child-victim, Pecola. And Morrison makes it clear that Pecola's father is not the only one who victimized her; justice is not served by putting him behind bars.[3] The entire black community of Lorain, Ohio, where Pecola's drama unfolds, is held accountable, as well as the larger forces of racism and the whites who practice it so casually and so devastatingly.

Morrison's lack of interest in the workings of the US justice system in her fictional worlds is less true of her nonfiction projects, as evidenced by her role as editor of two collections of essays on legal and ethical flashpoints in the tortured history of race in the US: *Race-ing Justice, En-Gendering Power: Essays on Anita Hill, Clarence Thomas, and the Construction of Social Reality* (1992) and *Birth of a Nation'hood: Gaze, Script, and Spectacle in the O. J. Simpson Case* (1997). Her disdain for the effectiveness of the justice system is evident in the introductions to both these collections and reinforces the stance she takes in her novels: that justice is rarely served when it comes to African Americans, whether as victims, perpetrators, or innocent bystanders.

In *Jazz* one of the main characters, Joe Trace, murders his lover, Dorcas, and not only does no one press charges against him, but the victim's one remaining family member, an aunt, develops a thorny but cathartic relationship with Joe's wife, Violet. Morrison's depiction of Joe is almost entirely sympathetic; he was a man who cheated on his wife because she had distanced herself from him; he killed the lover he took as a way of holding her. Morrison seems to absolve Joe of the murder when Dorcas's friend Felice blames Dorcas for letting herself die by refusing medical care. Dorcas's aunt, Alice Manfred, contemplates her niece's end:

> A man had come into her living room and destroyed her niece. His wife had come right into the funeral to nasty and dishonor her. She would have called the police after both of them if everything she knew about Negro life had made it even possible to consider. To actually volunteer to talk to one, black or white, to let him in her house, watch him adjust his hips in her chair to accommodate the blue steel that made him a man. (74)

Alice pursues a different kind of justice in an angry and satisfying truth-telling relationship with Joe's wife. Police and the law are shadowy figures in this story of love and murder.

In her introduction to *Birth of a Nation'hood*, Morrison addresses the role of police misconduct directly in her discussion of the O. J. Simpson case. She asserts that "police methods can alter perception in the construction of a public truth" (xxi). She continues:

[O]ne of the chief arguments in the Simpson case was whether police corruption was absurd or isolate. The story avoided as best it could whether corruption was endemic.... For whites to consider police corruption as systemic rather than occasional is to place themselves in the untenable position of being shielded *by*, rather than protected from, chaos.... The ordinary everyday experience of African Americans with the police is acknowledged, but since blacks and criminality are understood to go hand in hand, the outrage that should be the consequence of lawless police is muted. (xxi–xxii)

The focus of this collection of essays is on the false and damaging narratives created by the media storm surrounding the Simpson case. In her essay in the collection, Patricia J. Williams, a lawyer and legal scholar, also goes beyond limited legal constructions of the significance of the Simpson case. She examines the "odd silences and telling gaps in the media coverage of the post-O. J. moment" (277):

As black men continue to be Willie Horton-ized to death, no less do white women continue to be Nicole Brown Simpson-ized into the beautiful shape of the sheet-covered dead. Yes, Willie Horton was a real rapist and Nicole Brown Simpson was a real victim of domestic violence, but ... the public discussion turns him into all black men and her into all white women. (276)

Williams finally quotes Kimberlé Crenshaw in her work on intersectionality: "Underlying the legal parameters of racial discrimination are numerous narratives reflecting discrimination as it is experienced by black men, while the underlying imagery of gender discrimination incorporates the experience of white women" (277). Both lawyers, Williams and Crenshaw conceptualize American law as it should be or could be, and analyze false and damaging narratives of race and gender that distort legal outcomes.

In other writings Patricia J. Williams considers real-world issues of whether "justice too long delayed is justice denied," as Martin Luther King Jr. cautioned in his *Letter from Birmingham Jail*. In a discussion of the Justice Department's 2004 reopening of the Emmett Till case, Williams illuminates how the "dual justice system" of the Jim Crow South "corrode[d] the legitimacy of formal governance structures like the judiciary and render[ed] politics a farce." In other commentary on the reopening of the Till case, Margaret M. Russell, quoting the Justice Department's own language, asks, "what 'additional measure of justice' is possible after so many years.... What notions of 'justice' could be fulfilled today to compensate for so grievous a wrong?" (2106). The reopening of the Till case did not ultimately result in any legal action, but in 2007, the Emmett Till Act was signed by President George W. Bush, and it was expanded under President Barack Obama in 2016 to authorize the reopening of unsolved murders and other crimes from the civil rights era. In 2017 then–attorney general Jeff Sessions met with members of the Till family, and expressed a willingness to reopen the case once again, based on evidence of co-conspirators and an extraordinary retraction by Carolyn Bryant Donham, the woman who accused Till of grabbing and swearing at her in 1955, whose words prompted her husband and brother-in-law to brutally murder the fourteen-year-old Till.[4]

Real-world events enter the Morrisonian universe in a quick, sharp scene in Morrison's third novel, *Song of Solomon*, in which she introduces the Emmett Till story. Men gather at the barber shop to discuss the case.

> "He from the North," said Freddie. "Acting big down in Bilbo County. Who the hell he think he is?"
> "Thought he was a man, that's what," said Railroad Tommy.
> "Well, he thought wrong," Freddie said. "Ain't no black men in Bilbo County."
> "The hell they ain't," said Guitar.
> "Who?" asked Freddie.
> "Till. That's who." (81)

Other than Freddie, the men discussing the case are members of the Seven Days, a group of black men who "even the scales" of justice by killing white people whenever a black person is murdered and no one is held accountable. Morrison's exploration of the Seven Days' engagement in extralegal justice is at the center of *Song of Solmon*, but other than this scene and a few passing mentions of other civil rights era figures, she maintains a narrative distance from real-world events.

Morrison has not weighed in on the new developments regarding the Emmett Till case, but her disdain for the distorted popular narratives surrounding black criminality and the justice system is palpable in her scathing introductory essay to *Birth of a Nation'hood*. In her nonfiction Morrison takes on real-world issues head-on, here and in *Race-ing Justice*, but as a fiction writer she has no use for these false narratives. She turns away from the "real world" in seeming disgust and deliberately creates a separate fictional universe. Even the one courtroom scene in all her fiction, in *God Help the Child*, functions as a revelation of Bride's character, rather than as commentary on America's fraught and racially skewed courtrooms. In Morrison's fiction a formal justice system cannot heal the traumas of African American communities torn apart by slavery, Jim Crow, lynchings, endemic racism, and internalized racial self-hatred. Morrison's use of intertextual characters between her novels, as in *The Bluest Eye* and *God Help the Child*, emphasizes her disdain for formal justice and her fascination with characters existing in extranarrative spaces.

Extranarrative Spaces

Morrison certainly had Pecola and Pauline from *The Bluest Eye* in mind when she created the characters of Bride and her mother, Sweetness, in *God Help the Child*. Sweetness distances herself from her maternal role in the very name she gives herself in relation to her daughter. As she explains to the reader:

> I told her to call me "Sweetness" instead of "Mother" or "Mama." It was safer. Being that black and having what I think are too-thick lips calling me "Mama" would confuse people. Besides, she has funny-colored eyes, crow-black with a blue tint, something witchy about them too. (6)

It is significant that Bride's mother perceives "a blue tint" in her daughter's "funny-colored ... crow-black" and "witchy" eyes (6). As an adult, Bride is an exotic: a very black woman, rejected as un-look-at-able by her own mother, with blue-tinted eyes. In *The Bluest Eye*, Pecola attains her wished-for blue eyes, if only in her mind. Ultimately, the fate of these two dark-skinned girls with blue eyes, intertextually linked across Morrison's eleven novels, could not be more different.

In *God Help the Child*, Bride's witchy eyes with hints of blue take on a fantastical quality; as the novel progresses, Bride's pubic hair disappears, as do the piercings in her ears, and eventually her full, gorgeous breasts give way to a chest as flat as a washboard. Like the character Beloved, Bride's very physical form changes in reaction to emotional upheaval; unlike Beloved, who is after all a ghost, Bride, despite her witchy eyes, has no control over her physical transformations.

The symbolism of Bride's physical retreat into the body of a young girl is not hard to interpret; these physical changes correspond with an emotional crisis in which she uncovers the source of her cynicism and pain in her unfulfilled desire for an intimate connection with her distant mother. Also, considered intertextually, Bride becomes Pecola, in her bodily transformation to a young girl. Unlike Pecola, though, Bride is able to locate the source of her pain: her mother's withholding of love, manifested in an almost complete lack of physical touch. Bride remembers: "I used to pray she would slap my face or spank me just to feel her touch. I made little mistakes deliberately, but she had ways to punish me without touching the skin she hated" (31). Pecola, too young to analyze the disgust she feels from a white shopkeeper at the prospect of touching her hand when she pays for a piece of candy, too traumatized by her deeply damaged family, turns to fantasies of Shirley Temple and blue eyes to escape her pain and alienation. In contrast, Bride's awareness of why she hurts ensures she will survive her trauma.

As Bride overcomes her childhood trauma, she is also able to help her estranged lover, Booker, to confront and overcome his. This enables them to reunite in a close, authentic adult relationship. At least the reader hopes so. Morrison's seemingly pat catharsis, in which Bride and Booker face up to their own personal histories, including horrendous experiences of child abuse and murder, and come together soaked in the optimism of becoming parents together, is undercut by a final chapter in Sweetness's voice. She says, "You are about to find out ... how the world is" (178). Sweetness is undoubtedly an unreliable narrator; still, she serves the purpose of not allowing the reader to rest easy about Bride's newly acquired self-acceptance and smooth reunion with Booker.

Bride's pregnancy empowers her, while Pecola's pregnancy destroys her. The obvious reasons for this—Pecola's the result of rape by her own father, Bride's the result of a loving relationship—are problematized by Morrison's relentless portrayal of child abuse throughout both novels. *God Help the Child* portrays so many scenes of child sexual abuse that the reader cannot fully accept that a mere happy, consensual pregnancy between two damaged adults will take us to that elusive happy ending. And in *The Bluest Eye*, Pecola's rape is mirrored by the stories of children molested by the fake spiritualist Soaphead Church, as well as the furtive pawing of Pecola's friend Frieda by the family boarder.

Though Bride is not sexually abused, as Pecola was, she witnesses horrific sexual abuse as a young girl—she sees her landlord raping a little boy in the alley behind their apartment building. Worse, Bride's mother commands her to keep quiet about the abuse in order to stay on the landlord's good side. Bride keeps the secret into adulthood, finally sharing it with Booker. Unable to tell the secret of her landlord's horrible abuse, Bride's young self, little Lula Ann, finds another outlet for her trauma, which has the double benefit of gaining her mother's approval. Embroiled in a controversy at her elementary school in which two teachers are accused of child abuse, Lula Ann testifies against the teachers, describing terrible acts of sexual abuse in their trial. She transfers her traumatic witnessing of her landlord's sex crime to the teachers, and they are convicted and locked up for over a decade in a justice system gone awry.

Lula Ann's gratitude for her mother's approval of her testimony, expressed in a simple holding of hands, is fleeting, and the adult Bride is haunted by the consequences of her actions. She goes to meet one of the convicted teachers, Sofia Huxley, on the day of her release, offering her a large sum of money. She does not anticipate that the woman emerging from fifteen years in jail on a fabricated charge will react violently, but once Sofia attacks her, Bride does not fight back. She is badly injured but does not call the police. She does not turn to a justice system already shown to be irredeemably corrupt, in its unjust conviction of Sofia, to heal her wounds. Instead, she begins her own journey of becoming honest with herself about her own traumas.

A devastating consequence of Bride's decision to try to pay off the woman she put behind bars is that Booker leaves Bride quite suddenly. Over the course of the novel, we learn that it is Booker's own trauma of losing his brother to murder by a sexual predator that makes him abruptly end their relationship. The novel is a complicated web of adults and children working through their deepest personal traumas, sometimes with devastating effects, as with Lula Ann's false testimony.

Eventually, Bride and Booker shed the state of being defined by their traumas and come together lovingly. As Bride's wounds are healed, her woman's body returns—her ample breasts and body hair reappear. It is tempting to see her as a resurrected, healed Pecola.[5]

(No) Wrath

Bride's source trauma, predating her witnessing of a child-rape, can be traced back to her mother, Sweetness. Morrison never answers definitively how the high yellow Sweetness and her light-skinned husband came to be parents of a blue-black child. In Sweetness's last chapter, she speaks again of her disgust on seeing her dark-skinned baby: "True. I was really upset, even repelled by her black skin when she was born and at first I thought of . . . No. I have to push those memories away—fast. No point" (177; ellipsis in original). Sweetness could be referring to her abandoned attempt to smother her child, but she refers to "those memories"—plural, opening up the notion that she is also pushing away the memory of a dark-skinned man, not her husband, who fathered her child. The circumstances could have been traumatic—a rape. Or worse, from Sweetness's point of view, she could have *consented* to having sex with a very dark man. Repelled by her own desire for dark skin, Sweetness represses the memory of that desire and acts out her revulsion on her own child, believing no one can love a child that color.

In the penultimate chapter, Morrison allows her two main characters, Bride and Booker, to reunite and look forward optimistically to having a child together. She writes:

> [E]ach of them began to imagine what the future would certainly be....
>
> A child. New life. Immune to evil or illness, protected from kidnap, beatings, rape, racism, insult, hurt, self-loathing, abandonment. Error-free. All goodness. Minus wrath.
>
> So they believe. (175)

Morrison's use of the concept of wrath here is significant in light of her original title for the novel: *The Wrath of Children*. The original title serves as a crucial underlying theme of the novel, which Morrison signals early in Sweetness's voice: "What you do to children matters. And they might never forget" (43). Morrison's vision of the wrath of children is reinforced in the last chapter from Sweetness's point of view. Morrison does not allow her readers to buy into the gauzy vision of bliss imagined by Bride and Booker as they contemplate their impending parenthood. Instead, the final words of the novel are in Sweetness's cynical voice, addressing her estranged daughter:

> If you think mothering is all cooing, booties and diapers you're in for a big shock ...
>
> Listen to me. You are about to find out what it takes, how the world is, how it works and how it changes when you are a parent.
>
> Good luck and God help the child. (178)

Though she gives Sweetness the last word, Morrison is not endorsing this cynical vision. Sweetness's narration is consistently self-serving and unreliable. She is emotionally still a child, evidenced by her inability to enjoy her own motherhood, feeling it only as an enormous burden. She never progresses beyond her childlike assertion at the beginning of the novel, "It's not my fault" (3)—not her fault that her child's skin is so dark; not her fault that she couldn't love, or even touch, her own daughter; not her fault that her now-adult daughter no longer speaks to her. Giving Sweetness the literal last words of the novel does not give her the last word on the story Morrison is telling.

Morrison's tour de force novel of early slavery, *A Mercy*, also ends in the voice of the mother of the protagonist, Florens. We learn why this mother seemed to have abandoned her daughter by giving her away: she did it to save Florens from being reduced to sexual chattel, a state she herself is resigned to. Sixteen-year-old Florens's first-person narration sparkles with the wrath of an abandoned child; her need to understand her mother's abandonment is the driving force of *A Mercy* from its earliest pages. The construction of *A Mercy* leads the reader to accept this mother's vision as authoritative; it clarifies Florens's unanswered question about why her mother sent her away. Though a mother's voice also ends *God Help the Child*, this mother's vision does not have final authority. Readers are left unsettled by Sweetness's cynicism, but not convinced by it.

At the end of *The Bluest Eye*, Pecola, deep in her mental illness, mutters to herself and picks through a trash heap. The now-adult narrator, Claudia, asserts that Pecola is

> the waste and beauty of the world. . . . All of our waste which we dumped on her and which she absorbed. And all of our beauty, which was hers first and which she gave to us. All of us—all who knew her—felt so wholesome after we cleaned ourselves on her. We were so beautiful when we stood astride her ugliness. (205)

Bride, the blue-black woman with blue tints in her eyes, is the antidote to the devastation of Pecola. She is a so-called ugly girl who broke through, claimed her beauty, and embraced her blackness.

Blackness, in Morrison's vision, is never just about skin color. In describing her character Sula in her essay "Unspeakable Things Unspoken," Morrison writes:

> I always thought of Sula as quintessentially black, metaphysically black, if you will, which is not melanin and certainly not unquestion-

ing fidelity to the tribe. She is new world black and new world woman extracting choice from choicelessness, responding inventively to found things. Improvisational. Daring, disruptive, imaginative, modern, out-of-the-house, outlawed, unpolicing, uncontained and uncontainable. And dangerously female. [Sula] refers to herself as a special kind of black person woman, one with choices.... [a] double-dose of *chosen* blackness and *biological* blackness. (25–26; italics in original)

Sula's triumph of owning herself is bittersweet, however; she dies at thirty, having "sung all the songs that there are" (*Sula* 137). Bride's journey is more open-ended. She is a superficial success in the cosmetics industry, a woman who got rich by exploiting other women's insecurities. But within the world of Morrison's novels, her achievement of overcoming the color prejudice of the white world and the socially stratified colorism within the black world, by loving and embracing her blue-black self, is monumental. Bride overcomes what Pecola could not—she throws off her cloak of ugliness. She realizes it never even belonged to her.[6]

Morrison's disdain for traditional forms of justice crystalizes in characters in in-between spaces in her narratives: Pecola, Beloved, Wild, and finally Lula Ann, desperate for acceptance from her mother and also from the wider world. As the adult Bride, Lula Ann overcomes her need for acceptance from her mother by accepting herself. After Bride faces her traumas and enters into a loving, mature relationship with Booker, it is Sweetness who is exiled to the margin, waiting for attention, if only in the form of money, from her well-heeled daughter.

In Morrison's last published work, *The Source of Self-Regard*, she discusses in an essay of the same name where the characters in *Beloved* and *Jazz* derive their self-regard. In *The Bluest Eye*, Pecola has *no* source whatsoever to enable her to even begin to formulate a sense of self, while Bride in *God Help the Child* manages to find several: her profession, her grown-up love with Booker, the things she learns from other characters over the course of the novel. The arc from Morrison's first novel to her last, from the vulnerable and ultimately destroyed Pecola to the optimistic and healed Bride, tempts readers to see redemption for Pecola in Bride's rejection of racial self-hatred. There is no justice, but there is healing. But things are never that simple. Sweetness's cynical last chapter has the potential to upend Bride's newfound serenity. In typical fashion, Morrison leaves us at the end of the novel with fully explored, but not fully resolved, questions. There is no closure; the story is not over and must be told again in order to endure. With the loss of Morrison's voice at her passing in August 2019, we must rely on the many writers she has inspired to continue telling and retelling the ever-vital story of lost children, abandoning mothers, and the search for a healthy source of self-regard.

Notes

1. Morrison says, "Wild is a kind of Beloved. The dates are the same. You see a pregnant black woman naked at the end of *Beloved*.... The woman they call Wild ... could be Sethe's daughter, Beloved.... But I don't want to make all these connections" (Carabi 43).

2. Morrison explores colorism in her second novel, *Sula*, conveying its intricate rules in her dispassionate description of her two main characters:

> Nel was the color of wet sandpaper—just dark enough to escape the blows of the pitch-black truebloods and the contempt of old women who worried about such things as bad blood mixtures.... Had she been any lighter-skinned she would have needed either her mother's protection on the way to school or a streak of mean to defend herself. Sula was a heavy brown with large quiet eyes (52).

This description anticipates Morrison's exploration of the "eight-rock" community of "pure" blacks in *Paradise*, as well as Sweetness's unquestioning fidelity to the ideology of colorism.

3. Similarly, in *Beloved*, Sethe's brief trial and incarceration are incidental to Morrison's project of exploring the emotional and psychological toll of Sethe's murder of her baby. The fate of the real Margaret Garner, on whom Sethe's character is based, was quite different; she spent a significant time in jail, lost her trial, and was returned to slavery. Garner's trial was a cause célèbre for abolitionists of her era, but Morrison chose to deemphasize the legal consequences of her character's act of murder—Sethe's light sentence and return to free life are unrealistic and might be considered a flaw in the novel's plot if not for Morrison's masterful and convincing examination of Sethe's psychological breakdown.

4. Donham's retraction, given to historian Timothy Tyson in 2007 but only recently revealed, was first reported by Sheila Weller in *Vanity Fair* in January 2017.

5. At a Toni Morrison Society conference in July 2016, author John McCluskey related a conversation he'd had with Morrison. He asked, "How's Pecola?" Morrison

replied, "How'd you know?" to which McCluskey replied, "There's a Pecola in every town." Morrison told him, "She's fine. Has a couple of kids."

6. The Breedloves "wore their ugliness, put it on, so to speak, although it did not belong to them" (*Bluest Eye* 39).

Works Cited

Carabi, Angels. "Toni Morrison." *Belles Lettres: A Review of Books by Women*, vol. 10, no. 2, 1995, pp. 40–43.

Cutter, Martha J. "The Story Must Go On: The Fantastic, Narration, and Intertextuality in Toni Morrison's *Beloved* and *Jazz*." *African American Review*, vol. 34, no. 1, 2000, pp. 61–75.

Martínez Alfaro, María Jesús. "Intertextuality: Origins and Development of the Concept." *Atlantis*, vol. 18, no. 1–2, 1996, pp. 268–85.

Morrison, Toni, editor. *Birth of a Nation'hood. Gaze, Script, and Spectacle in the O. J. Simpson Case*. Pantheon, 1997.

———. *The Bluest Eye*. Knopf, 1970.

———. *God Help the Child*. Knopf, 2015.

———. *Jazz*. Knopf, 1991.

———. *Race-ing Justice, En-Gendering Power: Essays on Anita Hill, Clarence Thomas, and the Construction of Social Reality*. Pantheon, 1992.

———. *Song of Solomon*. Knopf, 1977.

———. *The Source of Self-Regard*. Knopf, 2019.

———. *Sula*. Knopf, 1973.

———. "Unspeakable Things Unspoken: The Afro-American Presence in American Literature." *Michigan Quarterly Review*, vol. 28, [Winter 1989]), pp. 1–34.

Russell, Margaret M. "Reopening the Emmett Till Case: Lessons and Challenges for Critical Race Practice." *Fordham Law Review*, vol. 73, no. 5, 2005, pp. 2101–32.

Tally, Justine. "Contextualizing Toni Morrison's Ninth Novel: What Mercy? Why Now?" *Toni Morrison's* A Mercy: *Critical Approaches*, edited by Shirley A. Stave and Justine Tally. Cambridge Scholars, 2011.

Weller, Sheila. "How Timothy Tyson Found the Woman at the Center of the Emmett Till Case." *Vanity Fair*, January 26, 2017. https://www.vanityfair.com/news/2017/01/how-author-timothy-tyson-found-the-woman-at-the-center-of-the-emmett-till-case?mbid=social_twitter.

Williams, Patricia. "Slow Motion: The Justice Department Recently Announced Its Intention to Reopen the Emmett Till case." *Nation*, May 27, 2004. https://www.thenation.com/article/slow-motion/.

About the Contributors

Alice Knox Eaton is professor of English and former Chair of the Humanities Department at Springfield College in Springfield, Massachusetts, where she teaches African American and Post-Colonial Literature. She contributed over a dozen biographical entries to the *African-American National Biography*, edited by Henry Louis Gates Jr., and has served as an officer and newsletter editor of the Toni Morrison Society. She has presented papers at several Society conferences, including the first international conference of the Society in Paris in November 2010. Her article "Becoming a She-Lion: Sexual Agency in Toni Morrison's *Beloved* and *A Mercy*" was published in the collection *Contested Boundaries: New Critical Essays on the Fiction of Toni Morrison*. In addition, she delivered a guest lecture at Worcester State University in October 2014 entitled "Bringing *Beloved* to Life: Sites of Slavery in Toni Morrison's Novels." She is currently at work on a project entitled "African American Culture and Autobiographical Criticism: A White Professor Explores Her Field."

Mar Gallego has taught American and African American Literatures at the University of Huelva (Spain) since 1996. She has been Director of the Research Center for Migration Studies at this University since 2011. She has been a Visiting Scholar at the Universities of Cornell (academic year 1991–92), Northwestern (1995, 2003, 2007, and 2011) and Harvard (1999, 2015, and 2016), and a lecturer in other countries, such as Ireland, Germany, Italy, Portugal, and Poland. Her major research interests are African American studies and the African diaspora, with a special focus on women writers and gender and migration issues. She has published two monographs entitled

Passing Novels in the Harlem Renaissance (Hamburg: LitVerlag, 2003), and *A ambas orillas del Atlántico: Geografías de hogar y diáspora en autoras afrodescendientes* (Oviedo: KRK, 2016). She has also coedited several essay collections: *Myth and Ritual in African American and Native American Literatures* (2001), *Contemporary Views on American Culture and Literature in the Great 60's* (2002), *Razón de mujer: Género y discurso en el ensayo femenino* (2003), *El legado plural de las mujeres* (2005), *Espacios de género* (2005), *Relatos de viajes, miradas de mujeres* (2007), *Género, ciudadanía y globalización* (2009 and 2011) and *The Dialectics of Diasporic Identification* (2009). Currently, she is completing a monograph on Toni Morrison's fiction that will soon be published.

Maxine Lavon Montgomery is the 2014–2017 Frances C. Ervin Professor of English at Florida State University, where she teaches courses in Africana Literature and Culture, Women's Literature and Culture, and American Multi-Ethnic Literature. Her articles have appeared in journals such as *African American Review*, *South Carolina Review*, *College Language Association Journal*, and the *Journal of Black Studies*. She is the author or editor of five books: *The Apocalypse in African-American Fiction* (UP of Florida, 1994); *Conversations with Gloria Naylor* (UP of Mississippi, 2004); *The Fiction of Gloria Naylor: Houses and Spaces of Resistance* (UP of Tennessee, 2010); *Contested Boundaries: New Critical Essays on the Fiction of Toni Morrison* (Cambridge Scholars, 2013); and *Conversations with Edwidge Danticat* (UP of Mississippi, 2017). Currently, she is at work on a book-length monograph on black women's speculative fiction.

Evelyn Jaffe Schreiber, PhD, is professor of English at The George Washington University. Her book *Subversive Voices: Eroticizing the Other in William Faulkner and Toni Morrison* examines identity and race via the theory of Jacques Lacan and cultural studies and was awarded the Toni Morrison Society book prize. It was a finalist for the MLA award for best first book, 2003. Her book *Race, Trauma, and Home in the Novels of Toni Morrison* is an interdisciplinary study of trauma in Morrison's fiction and was published in 2010. She teaches a course focused on Washington theater called "What's New about New Plays?" and a special course on race, identity, and trauma in William Faulkner and Toni Morrison. As a trained educator at the United States Holocaust Memorial Museum, she works with groups from the FBI, ICE, the State Department, state law enforcement, and schools.

Shirley A. (Holly) Stave is professor of Literature at the Louisiana Scholars' College at Northwestern State University. She has edited *Toni Morrison and the Bible: Contested Intertextualities*, and *Gloria Naylor: Strategy and Technique: Magic and Myth*, and coedited (with Justine Tally) *Toni Morrison's A Mercy: Critical Approaches*. She has contributed chapters to *The Cambridge Companion to Toni Morrison* (Ed. Justine Tally), *Toni Morrison: Memory and Meaning* (Ed. Adrienne Lanier Seward and Justine Tally), *Contested Boundaries: New Critical Essays on the Fiction of Toni Morrison* (ed. Maxine Montgomery), *Toni Morrison: Paradise, Love, A Mercy* (Ed. Lucie Fultz) and *Reading Texts, Reading Lives* (ed. Dan Morris and Helen Maxson). She is the author of *The Decline of the Goddess: Nature, Culture and Women in Thomas Hardy's Fiction* and has published on authors as diverse as Lee Smith and Wilkie Collins.

Justine Tally is professor of American Literature at the University of La Laguna (recently retired) where she has specialized in African American Literature and Culture. She is author of *Paradise Reconsidered: Toni Morrison's (Hi)stories and Truths* (Lit Verlag, 1999), *The Story of Jazz: Toni Morrison's Dialogic Imagination* (Lit Verlag, 2001), and *Toni Morrison's Beloved: Origins* (Routledge, 2009). She has edited the *Cambridge Companion to Toni Morrison* (CUP 2007) and coedited with Walter Hölbling *Theories and Texts* (Lit Verlag, 2007, 2009), with Shirley A. Stave *Toni Morrison's A Mercy: Critical Approaches* (CSP 2011), and with Adrienne Seward a volume of collected essays entitled *Toni Morrison: Memory and Meaning* (UP of Mississippi, 2014), winner of the Best Edited Book on Morrison for 2014–2015. She is also coeditor with Carmen Birkle of the section of E-JAS special issue on *Women in the USA*, vol. 10, no. 1 (2015), entitled "Waging Health: Women in Nineteenth-Century American Wars."

Susana Vega-González is associate professor at the University of Oviedo, Spain. She has published extensively on Toni Morrison as well as other African American and ethnic American writers. Her publications include the following articles and book chapters: "Literary Monuments: *Home* as a Commemorative Novel," "Orphanhood in Toni Morrison's *A Mercy*," "Toni Morrison's *Love* and the Trickster Paradigm," "A Comparative Study of Danticat's *The Farming of Bones* and Morrison's *Beloved*," "Writing Memory across the Borderline: Edwidge Danticat's and Julia Alvarez's Novels of Survival," and "Toward a Love Ethic: Love and Spirituality in bell hooks's Writing."

Anissa Janine Wardi is professor of English and African American Literature at Chatham University in Pittsburgh, Pennsylvania, and a past contributor to journals such as *African American Review*, *Callaloo*, *MELUS*, and *ISLE*. She is the author of *Death and the Arc of Mourning in African American Literature*, *Water*, and *African American Memory: An Ecocritical Perspective*. She is currently at work on a manuscript, *Toni Morrison and the Natural World: An Ecology of Color*.

Index

Abjection, 8–9
Akinyela, Makunga M., 35
Atkinson, Yvonne, 32

Ball, Philip, 96, 97, 100, 101
Banfield, Janet, 90
Banning, Mary, 103n4
Beloved, x, xii–xiii, 59, 61, 69, 89, 93–94, 103, 124, 127, 140, 142, 155; Amy Denver, 61; Baby Suggs, 69, 93–94; Beloved, 89, 114, 142, 150, 155; Denver, 28n3; Paul D, 103; Sethe, x, 59, 70, 93–94, 103, 109
Berg, Allison, 35
Berlant, Lauren, 23
Bhabha, Homi, 112
Birth of a Nation'hood: Gaze, Script, and Spectacle in the O. J. Simpson Case, 146–47
Blank, Art, 31, 45n3
Bluest Eye, The, x, xii–xiii, 27–28, 36, 51, 54, 59, 64, 66, 68, 71, 94, 96, 102, 124–25, 130, 140–45, 149–51, 154–55; Claudia McTeer, 94, 125, 140, 145, 154; Frieda McTeer, 125, 140, 145, 151; Lorain, Ohio, 143, 145; Pauline Breedlove, 109, 125, 144, 149; Pecola Breedlove, x, 6, 36, 59, 60, 62, 70, 96, 111, 115, 124–25, 127, 130, 140, 143–45, 149–52, 154–55
Brach, Tara, 81
Brogan, Kathleen, 114
Butler, Judith, 8, 14, 16, 25, 112

Caruth, Cathy, 43, 45n3
Cherry, Kendra, 138n11
Color, 90–97, 99, 102, 103nn1–4, 114, 116, 118n7
Color field painting, 95
Colorism, 5, 6, 7, 36, 50, 51, 96, 143, 144, 156n2
Collins, Patricia Hill, 24, 26, 48–49
Conner, Marc C., 45
Cooper, J. C., 33, 78, 79
Crenshaw, Kimberlé, 147
Cutter, Martha, 142–43

"Dancing Mind, The," 67
Delaunay, Sonia, 100
Denard, Carolyn, 68
Depth, 5, 11, 15, 17, 19, 24
Derridean Trace, 114
Diaspora, 108, 109, 110, 113, 114, 117, 159
Dillard, Sherrie, 78
Displacement, 135
Donato, Eugenio, 114

Eckstut, Arielle, 99
Eckstut, Joanne, 99
Erasure, 16, 32, 36, 38, 74, 107, 114, 115, 127, 128, 129, 130, 131, 133
Eudell, Demetrius L., 6

Fairy tale, 34, 59, 107, 115, 118nn2–6
Fanon, Frantz, 99, 111
Fatoumata, Keita, 59
Felman, Shoshana, 44

Fernanda, Moore, 50
Frankl, Victor, 83
Fultz, Lucille, 8, 9, 13
Furman, Jan, 59, 60

Gates, Henry Louis, 61
Gay, Roxane, 89
Gebuis, Titia, 90
God Help the Child: Adam, 21, 23, 24, 26, 43, 63, 81, 100, 101, 110, 112, 124, 128, 131, 133; Booker's shaving brush, 13, 19, 28n5, 99, 126; Bride's physical transformation, 39, 60–61, 73–74, 81, 117, 129, 134, 138nn18–20, 150; Brooklyn, 12, 30, 39, 52–54, 72, 100, 135; Evelyn, 18, 39–40, 61–62, 134; Hannah, 64n7, 116, 143; Julie, 59; Lula Ann, 9, 10, 18, 30, 35, 37, 38, 43, 50, 54–55, 60, 72, 129, 137n1, 144, 155; Queen Olive, 20–21, 26, 28n7, 40, 42, 73, 80–81, 115–16, 130, 136; Rain, 18–19, 40, 62, 63, 72–73, 78–79, 110, 130, 131, 132; Sofia, 15, 16, 26, 37–38, 55, 82, 83, 110, 126, 129, 134–35, 151–52; Steve, 18, 39, 61, 77; Sweetness, 7, 10, 27, 35–36, 44, 49–50, 58, 59–60, 71–72, 73, 96, 109, 124, 130, 143–44, 151, 152, 153–54

Hanh, Thich Nhat, 77, 84
Hartman, Geoffrey, 45nn2–3
Henderson, Mae, 7, 108
Herman, Judith, 49
Hoby, Hermione, 51
hooks, bell, 32, 58, 64n2
Home, 82, 110, 115; Cee Money, 70; Frank Money, 70, 115; Lotus, Georgia, 115
Hubert, Susan, 32
Hurston, Zora Neale, 5

Interpellation, 10
Intersectionality, 47–49, 147

Jones, Saeed, 89
Jazz, xii, 114, 124, 142, 146, 155; Dorcas, 146; Joe Trace, 146; Violet, 146; Wild, 114, 142, 155
Journey, 17, 36, 39, 47–48, 60, 63, 70, 76, 79, 81, 83, 107, 111, 113, 115, 117, 126–27, 152
Justice, 145–49, 151, 152, 155, 156

Kabat-Zinn, Jon, 70
Kristeva, Julia, 141

Lacan, Jacques, 9–10, 11, 32, 141; Mirror Stage, 11, 32; Name-of-the-Father, 9, 11, 14, 17; Objet a, 26, 28n5
La Capra, Dominick, 115
Langer, Suzanne, 91
Larson, Nella, 5
Lasch, Christopher, 135
Laub, Dori, 31, 32, 36
Lifton, Robert Jay, 31, 43, 44
López-Ramírez, Manuela, 58
Love, xii, 54, 114; Celestial, 114; Christine, xii, 54; Heed, xii, 54
Luce, Jim, 97, 98
Lutz, Helma, 49

Macksey, Richard, 114
Madame C. J. Walker (Sarah Breedlove), 137n1
McGuire, Danielle, 35
Masculinity, 24, 25, 48
Mercy, A, 109–10, 123, 141, 154; Florens, 154; Minha Mae, 109
Middle Passage, 108, 112, 114, 116
Mother Africa, 109
Mulvey, Laura, 12
Murray, J-Glenn, 33
Murray, Joddy, 91
Murray, Pauli, 49
Music, 25, 33–34, 42, 43, 80, 97, 98, 104n7, 112, 113, 114, 117, 124
Muyumba, Walton, 90

Index

Nature, 70, 76, 77
Nijboer, Tanja C., 90

Origin of Others, The, 71, 110, 116
Orphans, 10, 27n2, 79, 110
Ovid, 107, 108, 111, 112, 118

Paradise, x, 6, 89–90, 110, 124; Connie, 137n7; Ruby, Oklahoma, 6, 124
Pedophilia, 15, 21, 23, 24, 48, 54, 55, 56, 57, 100, 123, 129, 151
Peretti, Burton, 34
Picasso, Pablo, 97
Playing in the Dark: Whiteness and the Literary Imagination, 109, 114

Quest motif, 130, 133, 135, 136

Race-ing Justice, En-Gendering Power: Essays on Anita Hill, Clarence Thomas, and the Construction of Social Reality, 146, 149
Rain (in nature), 11, 78, 79, 131
"Recitatif," 110
"Remarks Given at the Howard University Charter Day Convocation," 68
Rentzenbrink, Cathy, 82
Richardson, Jim, 102
Rifkind, Donna, 89
"Rootedness: The Ancestor as Foundation," 114
Roynon, Tessa, 107
Russell, Margaret M., 148

Selfhood, 17, 130
Sexism, 49, 52, 53, 54, 60
Showalter, Elaine, 123
Siegel, Daniel, 81
Silence, 37, 67–71, 77–78, 82–83, 103n6
Silverman, Kaja, 32
Smitherman, Geneva, 32
Spillers, Hortense, 6

Song of Solomon, 76, 89, 92, 115, 140, 148; Guitar, 148; Hagar, 124; Macon Dead, 124; Milkman, 76, 115, 124; Pilate, 82n2; Seven Days, 148–49; Shalimar, 115
Source of Self-Regard, The, 155
Stamberg, Susan, 95
Sula, xii, 124, 135, 140, 155; Eva Peace, 109, 124; Hannah Peace, 59, 110, 116, 124, 129, 136; Nel Wright, xii; Shadrack, 70; Sula Peace, xii, 89, 112, 136, 154–55
Surface, 5, 11, 12, 15, 17, 19, 22, 24

Tar Baby, 77, 90, 124, 140; Jadine, 77, 124, 140; Son, 140
Testimony, 30–35, 37, 38, 41, 43, 44
Thurman, Robert, 67
Till, Emmett, 148–49
Twagilimana, Aimable, 57

"Unspeakable Things Unspoken," 106, 154–55
Urist, Jacoba, 91

Van der Hart, Onno, 31–34
Van der Kolk, Bessel, 45n3, 74, 75, 80, 83
Van der Smagt, Maarten J., 90
Visvis, Vikki, 34

Wagner-Martin, Linda, 59, 60
Walker, Kara, 89
Waller, Fats, 98, 103n3
What Moves at the Margin, 83
Williams, Kidada, 34
Williams, Patricia J., 147, 148
Williams, Tennessee, *The Rose Tattoo*, 24, 124, 135, 136, 137
Wright, Cuffee, 33
Wyatt, Jean, 8, 19, 27, 27n2, 132, 133–34, 137n8, 138n12